HAUNTED YORK

A GUIDED WALK AROUND
THE STREETS AND TAVERNS OF

HAUNTED YORK

VINCENT DANKS

HALSGROVE

First published in Great Britain in 2018

British Library Cataloguing-in-Publication Data
A CIP record for this title is available from the British Library

ISBN 978 0 85704 333 7

HALSGROVE
Halsgrove House,
Ryelands Business Park,
Bagley Road, Wellington, Somerset TA21 9PZ
Tel: 01823 653777   Fax: 01823 216796
email: sales@halsgrove.com
www.halsgrove.com

Printed in India by Parksons Graphics

INTRODUCTION

To the most haunted city in Europe ...

While the accuracy of the above accolade may be disputed by other haunted cities in Europe, what cannot be denied is that the sheer volume of documented sightings ranks York as one of the most haunted cities in the world.

Founded in AD 71 the city has continually been regarded as an important military and administrative base, with the consequence of playing host to a number of different invaders. For the Romans, whose ghostly legacy has created one of the best known sightings in the country (see page 14), York, or Eboracum as they named it, was established and developed as a military strongpoint and excavations of remains, including a bath, temple and Roman bridge are still continuing today.

The Minster, with its variety of manifestations (see page 63), is England's largest mediaeval cathedral and one of Europe's largest gothic churches. It was originally built in 627, although possibly on a different site. In 866 the city fell prey to the invading Vikings, who renamed it Jorvik and ruled the area for nearly a hundred years until expelled by the Anglo-Saxons.

The late mediaeval period saw prosperous growth and much of the building work, such as the city walls and their entrance gates (known as bars) survive to this day. The old butchers' street known as Shambles dates from about the same period and although now home to gift shops rather than meat sellers it's one of the most atmospheric places in the city.

This book has been designed to guide you around the best known locations of spectral manifestations and also, where it has been possible without leading you too far astray from the haunted trail, to reveal some of York's hidden streets and buildings and give you a feel for the historical legacy that is the backdrop to our otherworldly inhabitants.

CONTENTS

INTRODUCTION 5
GUIDE TO THE MAPS 8

WALK ONE
MAP – page 10
Haunted York

Precentor's Court • Treasurer's House • Grays Court • St William's College • College Street • Bedern • St Saviour • Clifford's Tower • The York Barguest • York Castle Museum • York Dungeon • Priory Church of the Holy Trinity • Micklegate Bar • Guildhall • Judge's Court • All Saints' Church • Shambles • Holy Trinity Church • Stonegate • Yorkshire Museum • King's Manor • York Theatre Royal • The Minster

WALK TWO
MAP – page 66
Haunted Taverns

Hole in the Wall • The Royal Oak • The Golden Slipper • The Black Swan • Golden Fleece • Cock and Bottle • The Whippet Inn • Lendal Cellars • The Punchbowl • Ye Olde Starre Inne • Roman Bath • Old White Swan • Snickleway Inn • The Guy Fawkes Inn • Dean Court Hotel • York Arms

WALK THREE
GEORGE CROWQUILL PURKESS ESQ 88

The Ghosts of York • York Castle Museum • Wade & The Witch and & Hand From Ol' Nick • The Red Devil • The Haunting of Laurence Sterne • Thomas Gent

THE EBOR GHOST 103
THE COMMON HALL LANE GHOST 104

ASIDES

A64 Malton Road 18
Foss Bridge 27
Dick Turpin's Grave 31
St George's Field 33
River Ouse 33

Bishopthorpe 34
National Railway Museum 42
St Crux Church 45
Davygate 49
Lund's Court – Formerly Mad Alice Lane 52
Clifton Lodge 62
The Four Alls Inn 71

DON'T STRAY FROM THE PATH

Toy Shop Just Inside Roman Gate 19
Spen Lane... 24
Castlegate House 33
St Mary's Church 34
Coppergate Shops... 36
Bar Convent.. 41
St Mary's Abbey... 58
St Michael le Belfrey 62
The Watergate Inn 74
The Windmill Inn.. 77

COMPLETE WALK
MAP – page 106
Every haunted location that features in the three walks,
combined into a single journey.

EPILOGUE 112

GUIDE TO THE MAPS

Where to Begin ...

Where possible, all the individual walks detailed in the maps will guide you around the locations without the potentially tedious occurrence of re-visiting the same area more than once. It will happen occasionally but we sincerely hope that our hard work in keeping this to a minimum will not in any way impair your enjoyment of the overall experience.[1]

The maps will all start you at a particular locale and we have ensured that you will be guided back to that spot at the culmination of your journey. This should empower you with a sense of reassurance that as you head into the darker elements of York's streets and back alleys you will not be lost forever.

At this point, and without wishing to sound too alarmist, I urge you to not stray from the designated path. Having said that, for the more adventurously inclined amongst you there are a number of 'asides' detailed throughout the book that will also be marked on the maps. These can be visited with small detours from the paths and you should not find it too difficult to re-join your original route.

All the walks start you in the vicinity of Bootham Bar, itself the location of a decidedly contemporary apparition in the form of a gentleman attired in a polo shirt and shorts. More traditionally, the sighting of a nun was also reported in the 1970s, attired in a rather tattered brown habit and walking in the direction of the Bar. After a short while she vanished and it may well be that she was headed, depending on the direction she was going, in either the direction of the York Theatre Royal (see page 61) or the York Arms (see page 87).

Bootham Bar is one of four main gatehouses that are part of the enclosing wall that surrounds the city. These and a number of minor bars are illustrated on the maps.

MAP ONE
HAUNTED YORK
The best known stories and their accompanying places of residence along with a wondrous trip through York's historic streets and snickets.

MAP TWO
HAUNTED TAVERN GUIDE
Resisting the temptation to indulge in a witty reference to spirits this guide will introduce you to not only some of the best ghost stories that York has to offer but also some of its finest hostelries.

MAP THREE
THE COMPLETE WALK

With the exception of the asides, this will guide you around every location that features in the book, including those detailed in Mr Crowquill's articles, taking in all the streets, buildings, pubs and people that are the rich tapestry of York's spectral geography.

THE ASIDES

As the title implies, these are not part of the walks for a variety of reasons, including location, lack of decent information concerning the subject matter and an inability on our part to decide where to put them. However, they are all either ghost related or at the very least a bit odd so we've included them for you to either embrace enthusiastically or reject emphatically. Entirely a matter for your own consideration.

DON'T STRAY FROM THE PATH

Similar in spirit (apologies) to the asides, these are nuggets of information that have been included so as to allow those who appreciate them an opportunity to investigate. All are within easy reach of the main walks and you should not, all being well, have any trouble finding your way back onto the main path.

*Note of Caution!

Please be aware that York is notorious for its ability to flood at the drop of a piece of water so, depending on the time of year of your visit, it may be necessary to adapt your route at certain junctures so as to avoid being taken by the Kelpies.

WALK ONE

Haunted York

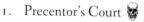

1. Precentor's Court
2. The Treasurer's House
3. Grays Court
4. St William's College
5. 5 College Street
6. Bedern
7. St Saviour
8. Clifford's Tower
9. The York Barguest
10. York Castle Museum
11. York Dungeon
12. Priory Church of the Holy Trinity

13. Micklegate Bar
14. Guildhall
15. Judge's Court
16. All Saints' Church
17. Shambles
18. Holy Trinity Church
19. Stonegate
20. The Yorkshire Museum
21. The King's Manor
22. York Theatre Royal
23. York Minster

Asides

1. A64 Malton Road
2. Foss Bridge
3. Dick Turpin's Grave
4. St George's Field
5. Bishopthorpe
6. Edge of the River Ouse

7. National Railway Museum
8. St Crux Church
9. Davygate
10. Lund's Court – formerly Mad Alice Lane
11. Clifton Lodge

Don't stray from the path

1. Toy Shop / Roman Gate
2. Spen Lane
3. Castlegate House
4. St Mary's Church
5. Coppergate Shops
6. Bar Convent
7. St Mary's Abbey
8. St Michael le Belfrey

A GUIDED WALK
ROUND THE STREETS
AND TAVERNS OF

HAUNTED YORK

Where you begin...

Having located Bootham Bar (unless you were tempted to start with the haunted pub walk, in which case you already know where it is) head down High Petergate towards the Minster and the street will be broken by the formidable edifice that is York Minster.

Running to the right of the Minster is Minster Yard, which runs into Deangate, now pedestrianised as a result of concerns that the traffic might cause the old church to fall down. Turn to your left and walk along the slightly curved row of buildings that face the Minster until you reach the base of the street that begins our haunted journey.

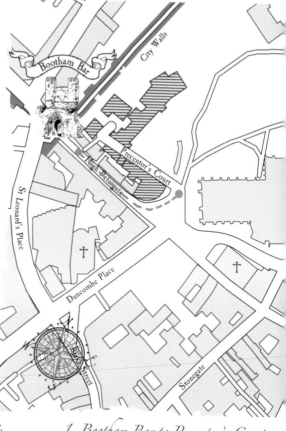

1. Bootham Bar to Precentor's Court

PRECENTOR'S COURT

*M*J. Wayland[1] recounts an eerie tale from the beginning of the last century that followed the digging up of a large number of human remains while undertaking work on a new drainage system. Bones being dug up from under and around the Minster appear to be a common occurrence, including a pair of feet dated from the eleventh century, and therefore Viking, found when the undercroft was excavated in 2012, and a pre Norman Conquest cemetery was discovered under the south transept of York Minster in the late sixties.

It transpires that on a certain winter's evening during this period a young woman was visiting one of the residences in Precentor's Court and, not unreasonably, took to knocking upon the door of said home. Not receiving an answer she continued her labour until the door swung open and revealed the inside of the property to be consumed with fire. Standing amidst this inferno was a young girl, and as the scene before her appeared to grow and fill the entire doorway the woman was so terrified that she ran to a neighbour's house to gain some refuge. There she was informed that the property had been uninhabited for over a month due to the residents being away. Apparently there are no further details as to the nature of the experience and one can only hope that the poor woman recovered her wits and was able to put the matter from her mind.

An interesting detail about No 1 Precentor's Court, the house that will be right next to you as you gaze up the street, is that the basement of the property has a window in one of the walls. An odd feature in itself you would imagine but particularly unnerving is that visible through the window are a row of ancient arches looming out of the darkness. One can't help but wonder what else would appear if the window was watched for any length of time.

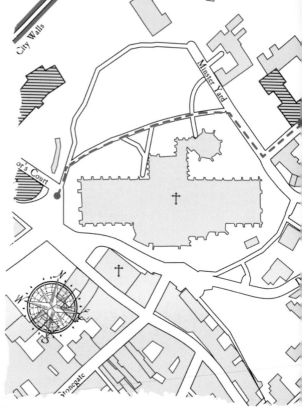

When leaving Precentor's Court you will see to your left the entrance to Deans Park. Follow one of the two paths to its conclusion and you will emerge onto Minster Yard, where, just a short stroll along, will be the impressive frontage of our next spectral encounter.

2. Precentor's Court to the Treasurer's House

TREASURER'S HOUSE

You will, however, need to take the first turning left into Ogleforth and then find the doorway in the wall to gain entry.

Sitting in the shadow of York Minster, the Treasurer's House is as important for its history as it is notorious for its ghosts. Built on a Roman site and originally the mediaeval home of the Minster's Treasurer, the house was all but destroyed in the great fire of York in 1137[1] (perhaps a clue as to the nature of the Precentor's Court story).

Following Henry VIII's Reformation of the English Church in the 1540s the post of Treasurer was abolished, resulting in the highly indignant exiting Treasurer William Cliff remarking that as the Minster had been plundered of all its treasures it had no further need of a Treasurer. As such, the house passed into the hands of the Archbishops of York.

By the seventeenth century it had become a far more secular dwelling and was purchased by the prospering George Aislaby from Lord Fairfax in 1663. By the time

the fateful night of 10 January 1647 came about George Aislaby and his wife were established enough to be invited, along with Mrs Aislaby's sister Mary Mallorie, to the Duke of Buckingham's ball in Skeldergate. At the party, Mary Mallorie met up with her fiancée, Jonathon Jennings, an entirely appropriate arrangement were it not for the subsequent fact that they failed to return to the Treasurer's House later that night.

The family's honour clearly impeached, George Aislaby challenged Jennings to a duel which took place on the Sunday morning. At the stroke of the Minster's prayer bell they went at each other with swords. the result being a mortally wounded Aislaby. Buried nearby, his supernatural presence is particularly strong around the Chapterhouse Street entrance.

A further violent altercation, this time between a previous owner and his wife, followed the husband's threat to move his mistress into the house. This not unreasonable reaction from the lady of the house is said to have resulted in a cold and foreboding atmosphere in the Tapestry room on the first floor, a room that subsequently became the location of a manifestation in more recent times.

15

A volunteer worker at the house was checking her hair in the room's somewhat dilapidated mirror when a woman dressed in black appeared in the reflection, staring at her. Suitably unnerved she turned around to find the room quite unoccupied with the exception of herself. Upon returning her gaze to the mirror the woman was still there. In addition to a spectral hound and a black cat, the most intriguing and certainly the best known apparitions wandering around the Treasurer's House are the Roman soldiers that appear in the cellar. A young apprentice plumber by the name of Harry Martindale created intense interest when he made some notable observations about the ghosts that were at odds with most people's pre-conceived ideas about Romans. Working in the cellar in the early 1950s Harry's encounter began with the sound of a trumpet blast, followed by the appearance of a Roman on horseback and a procession of foot soldiers. Unlike the shining and disciplined soldier of Hollywood movies,

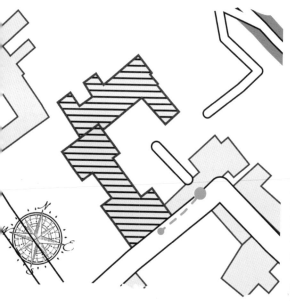

3. Treasurer's House to Grays Court

these men were dirty and unkempt with a weary look that suggested they had returned from a long journey. Although frightened and unsure of the nature of his experience Harry was able to take in a number of details that imbued his testimony with a great deal of verity. The poor quality of their clothing, the cross-gartering of their sandals, round shields and the green kilted skirts they were wearing were all features that, although known to be historically correct, were not familiar to people outside academic circles.

In addition, Harry noticed that the soldiers were not visible below their knees. That is, until they reached a section of the cellar where the original Roman road, lying eighteen inches below the cellar floor, had been recently excavated. With no apparent awareness of the presence of the young man watching in amazement at their passing, the Romans vanished into the wall at the opposite side of the cellar.

Such is the notoriety of the late Harry Martindale's story that there is a small exhibition room in the Treasurer's House containing a videoed interview with the man and should the idea take your fancy you can watch this prior to visiting the actual basement itself.

When exiting the Treasurer's House, turn left and walk a few paces up Ogleforth and on your left will be the entrance to an establishment that proudly proclaims to be the oldest inhabited house in York and one that surprisingly, certainly given how fabulous the place is, remains one of York's hidden gems.

GRAYS COURT

Originally part of the Treasurer's House, both properties have undergone extensive changes over the centuries and the present Grays Court owes much of it's disposition to Dr Jaques Sterne, the uncle of the famous Laurence Sterne (see page 99) who built the Sterne Room and also subdivided the property, subsequently selling what is now the north wing of the Treasure's House to Francis Topham. William Gray and his family bought and occupied part of the house until 1945 and it is to them that building owes its name and further alterations including a new staircase in the middle of the gallery.

For a while Grays Court was owned by the Dean and Chapter and leased by St John's College but is now, after much trial, tribulation and the death of one of the couple who bought the property, a boutique hotel[1]. With it's troubled history it is perhaps inevitable that there are ghosts. A gentleman has been seen attired in Victorian clothing and it has been suggested that he is the ghost of George Aislabie, also resident spook at the Treasurer's House. Given the shared history and close proximity of the two buildings this would seem a reasonable assumption were it not for the fact that George lived and died in the seventeenth century, so unless the spirit realm is in the habit of keeping up with changing fashion it would seem unlikely that he would materialise dressed as a Victorian.

An additional phantom figure has been witnessed in the form of an indistinct and green-hued woman who takes to walking up and down the main staircase. Perhaps wisely, her identity has not even been speculated upon.

A64 MALTON ROAD

A number of ghostly manifestations in York are connected to, or are actual sightings of, either Dick Turpin (see page 31) or an unidentified highwayman.

This relatively recent report in April 2010[i] is no exception, and is of particular note for taking place in the same vicinity as a second highwayman sighting at the Four Alls Inn (see page 71). The witness apparently saw a young woman walking along the A64 in the direction of Malton carrying a child, The report states that the witness felt that they were the victim of a highwayman, possibly the woman's boyfriend.

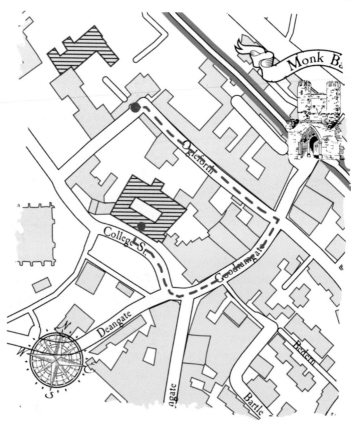

4. Grays Court to St William's College

*A*s you walk back out of Grays Court, continue straight ahead until you reach the end of Ogleforth. Turn right into Goodramgate, past the Royal Oak and Golden Slipper pubs (see page 69) on your right and before long the ever-present Minster will appear before you. Take a right turn under the medieval archway that is the last remaining of the original four entrances into the Minster precinct (see page 69) and you will be in College Street. After a short stroll you will see to your right the building that gives its name to the street and our next ghostly subject.

St William's College

*B*uilt in 1461 and named after St William of York, the nephew of King Stephen, St William's College is a beautiful stone and timber-framed building constructed for the purpose of providing accommodation for priests serving chantries[1] in the Minster.

In the first half of the seventeenth century it became the home of the printing presses of King Charles I during England, Scotland and Ireland's first civil war.

TOY SHOP JUST INSIDE ROMAN GATE

There are a number of references to this sighting and they all refer to the location in this rather indistinct way. The experience reported may actually have been a time-slip rather than a ghost sighting as the witness made a reference to being in an altered state of consciousness. Even more curious is that her point of view also altered so that she witnessed her surroundings from the vantage point of the ghost.

The experience occurred late one night as a teddy bear in the toy shop window caught our subject's attention and she moved closer to get a better view. Once at the window her perspective changed and she transformed into a baker working inside the shop. Looking up from her work she could see Roman soldiers outside, walking past the window.

There is a toy shop in York that is just inside Monk Bar, although in reality it's a railway and plastic kit model shop, which itself is situated a mere one hundred metres from the site of the old Roman fortress. In addition, the line of Monkgate itself is thought to be the approximate site of an old Roman road running north east.

Could this be the location of a most extraordinary encounter with the past?

19

However, the resident ghost is thought to date from the time of the clergys' occupation of the building when it is reputed that two brothers who lived among the upper rooms had murdered a fellow priest. In an act of self preservation the eldest brother had informed the authorities and told them that they would find his sibling hiding in an oak closet within one of the rooms. On returning to the college the man felt somewhat guilt-ridden about this act of treachery and paced the corridors of the building in an agitated state of shame and regret. The authorities finally showed up and duly extracted the younger sibling from his hiding place and hanged him for the crime.

The elder brother, having given evidence against him, was spared the same fate. However, a worse fate awaited him as his guilt was such that he has been witnessed pacing the corridors, his soul condemned to an eternal state of distress.

Interestingly, there is a further, postscript story as chronicled in the *The Wortlebank Diary* by Holme Lee published in 1860. Associated with the building's later use once it had been converted into rented apartments, it is that rare thing amongst true ghost tales: a sequel!

An engraver by the name of Nicholas Drew occupied a complete floor in the upper part of the college and during a particularly cold and snowy New Year's Eve he found a young girl crying in the courtyard porch of the college. A fellow tenant identified the child as belonging to a woodcarver who also lived within the college building. On discovering the father dead, Nicholas resolved to keep the child and raise her as his own.

Many years later Nicholas and his adopted daughter, now a woman, argued over the attentions being paid to her by a humourless character by the name of Laurence Royston. On forbidding any contact between them Royston paid the father a visit and an angry confrontation led to Nicholas being murdered. Next to the bloody body of the man he had just killed, Royston noticed a large oak cabinet, a cabinet that had allegedly belonged to the very brothers who had murdered the priest. Deciding to make the death look like the work of thieves Royston broke into the cabinet and pulled out its contents.

His subterfuge complete, Royston then began a hasty exit from the building, but after entering the main room of the apartment, he was confronted by the sound of heavy footsteps, slow and unmistakable, moving towards him. Fearing his dreadful act may have been discovered, Royston looked nervously around the room for the source of the footsteps, however, besides himself and the dead

Nicholas in the adjacent room, the apartment was completely empty.

*A*s you make your own (possibly hasty) retreat from the ancient building you must continue along College Street until you are almost at the foot of the east end

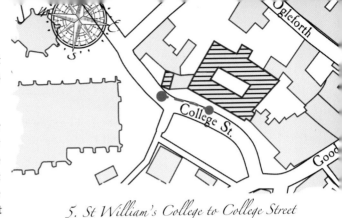

5. St William's College to College Street

of the Minster. As it towers above you, look to your right and at the end of the line of houses is our next haunted encounter.

COLLEGE STREET

*W*ith the Minster towering above it to the left, the fifteenth century timber building of St William's College to the right and the Treasurer's House just round the corner, number 5 College Street is situated in the most densely haunted area in the whole of the city. As if that wasn't enough, the house itself dates back to medieval times and it therefore comes as little surprise to learn that it has a resident ghost. Arguably what does cause a certain amount of disbelief is the fact that there is only one.

The phantom in question owes its existence to a miserable and somewhat harrowing tale of a young girl who died of starvation during the Great Plague of 1604, a plague which killed 3512 people in a city whose population was only around 10,000.

The details of her story emerged following a requested seance by a family occupying the house in the early part of the twentieth century. People over the years had often complained of an intense sadness that pervades the house but the two children living there at this time were troubled by a continual crying, footsteps running around the upstairs part of the house and the materialisation, also seen by the nanny, of a young girl in an old-fashioned white dress.

The seance revealed that the girl's parents had both died of the plague. Their servants, inevitably lacking the medical skills required to make an accurate diagnosis, mistakenly believed that the daughter, also stricken with the illness, had died along with them. As such, they left the property to be boarded up in line with plague regulations that were designed to isolate infected areas. However, the girl recovered and awoke to find herself abandoned with her dead parents. Small wonder that her ghostly presence should manifest itself as agitated footprints and the sobbing of a lonely, helpless child.

It is perhaps for the best that we quickly turn away from this ancient residence and take in the full majesty of the east face of the Minster, by way of a calming moment or two before heading towards our next chilling destination.

I f we re-trace our steps along College Street, back under the archway and turn left into Goodramgate you will see another archway that marks the entrance to our next spook infested location.

BEDERN

O ne of the more harrowing tales behind York's catalogue of ghostly sightings has its location around the small selection of streets know as Bedern, situated between Goodramgate and the now decidedly posh street of St Andrewgate.

Meaning 'House of Prayer', Bedern was once a square and the home to the College of the Minister's Vicars Choral. The college refectory, or dining hall, is still standing and is currently hired out for private functions (sadly, the bridge which used to link the hall with Minster Close no longer exists)[1].

When the Vicars' moved out of the square in 1574 the area slowly degenerated and by the end of the eighteenth century a predominantly Irish population was surviving in what was described by T. Whellan[2] as a 'sad spectacle of poverty and wretchedness'.

Within this area stood a house that had been used as an old people's home since 1575. In 1847 the residents were moved out and the building became the York

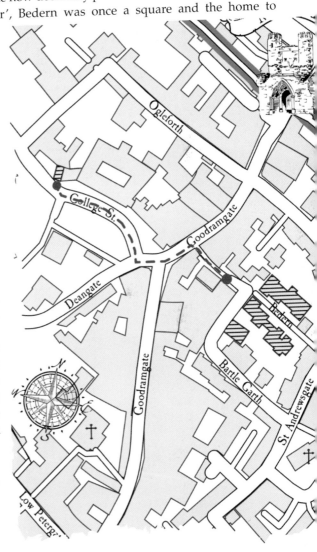

6. College Street to Bedern

Industrial Ragged School, whose master, in the true spirit of Dickens' child catcher, was tasked with the responsibility of rounding up the homeless children of York and, under his care, setting them to work. It became apparent that the man was more interested in the level of his income than the welfare of the children and the money that was intended for food and clothing for those in his charge was kept for himself, with the result that many of the children died of starvation or exposure. During warmer weather he would bury the dead in shallow graves but in winter, when the ground became too hard to dig, he would hide the bodies in a large cupboard and leave them to rot. In time, the mounting bodies and increased consumption of alcohol resulted in him hearing screams from the padlocked cupboard and before long his wretched state drove him to murder the remaining living children with a knife. He was arrested and committed to an asylum where he lived out the remainder of his life.

Bedern has been extensively developed in the years since those children's wretched lives came to an end but that has not stopped people reporting the feeling of a small child taking them by the hand as they walk through the archway and the ghostly sound of their playing, with the chilling addition that if one stops to listen, the playful noise soon becomes the sound of screaming.

SPEN LANE

The ultimate destination of the figure seen originating from the site of the now demolished St Crux church.

For more details, see page 45.

7. *Bedern to St Saviour*

urn right into Bartle Garth, follow it to its conclusion and it will bring you out onto the aforementioned St Andrewgate. Straight ahead of you is a small snicket that will lead you into Spen lane. Emerging from the snicket, walk straight ahead for a minute or two and take the first turning right into St Saviourgate. After a further short walk you will see on the left our next spectral destination.

SAINT SAVIOUR

aving already taken in the historical majesty of a number of haunted sites, it will come as no surprise by this point in the walk that St Saviour is an extremely old building. Built in the fifteenth century there are still parts of the original eleventh century church within its structure and it is a sad fact that although highly popular in the nineteenth century, by the dawn of the twentieth the parish was in such decline that it sat on the fringes of the worst slum area in York. As such, it was shut down and stripped of its contents and remained unused until the York Archaeological Trust bought it in 1975 and developed their 'Dig' attraction.

Given that the Trust were responsible for the retrieval of the artefacts underneath what is now the Jorvik centre, it seems eminently appropriate that St Saviour be haunted by the phantom of a Viking. The legend speaks of the poor chap being skinned alive by the Christian residents of York, possibly one of a number of acts of retribution following the Battle of Fulford Cross in 1066. Although this seems somewhat un-Christian behaviour, especially given that the Vikings had occupied York for 200 years before St Saviour was even built, it is possible that, bearing in mind that eleventh century stone, our would-be spectral Norwegian was murdered in a newly built church.

Equally tragic is the story of a ghost hunter who took it upon himself to undertake an all night vigil of St Saviour in an attempt to confirm the existence of our ill-treated Norseman. The tale presumably takes place prior to its closure as a church as it is the vicar who finds the hapless gentleman the following morning, apparently having died as a result of terror and lodged in one of the church's high beams.

An opportunity to steady your nerves will now present itself as we have a slightly longer stroll to our next destination which will hopefully serve you in good stead as there will be not one but three ghostly horrors all within the same vicinity.

FOSS BRIDGE

A woman, sometimes reported as wearing a shroud, has been seen walking down Fossgate from the direction of the site of the now demolished St Crux church. Upon reaching the bridge that spans the River Foss she vanishes.

It has been suggested that this may be the same ghost that has been seen leaving the same location of St Crux but heading in the opposite direction towards Spen Lane, where once again she disappears.

*C*ontinuing up St Saviourgate you should turn left at the end and then cross over Stonebow into Fossgate and before long you'll be going over a small bridge spanning the River Foss. Once over, take a right into Merchantgate and you'll see a Tesco Express ahead of you. To the right of that is a footway that will take you along the river towards our next supernatural experience.

CLIFFORD'S TOWER

*T*he sight of one York's bloodiest and most shameful episodes, the tower that sits atop the conical motte is the remnent of York Castle, built in 1270 to replace the wooden castle that was destroyed by fire. It is known as Clifford's Tower following the execution of Roger de Clifford, who was hung in chains from the walls in 1322 for treason against Edward II and left hanging there for a year and a day. His spectral form has been seen a number of times over the centuries and he persistently manifests even to this day.

The original castle was built by William the Conqueror in 1068 but was burnt during an uprising the following year. Its replacement was also burnt following a horrifying event that resulted in the massacre of 150 Jews inside the castle and the death of almost fifteen hundred people during anti-Semitic riots in 1190. Two leaders of York's Jewish

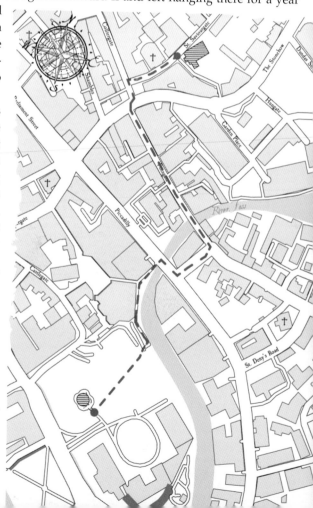

8. St Saviours to Clifford's Tower

community, Benedict and Jocencus, had travelled to London for the coronation of King Richard but were attacked upon their return to such an extent that Benedict died of his injuries. His house was looted and his wife and children murdered. Jocencus and a large group of his fellow citizens were given permission by the Constable of York Castle to take refuge within the castle but a large mob, incited by the cries of a monk dressed in white, attacked the walls and a number of the trapped Jews committed suicide rather than be taken by the large Christian horde. The survivors opened the doors and begged for mercy, offering large amount s of money for their lives. Their pleas were ignored and the rioters murdered every one of them and set the castle ablaze.

Each spring, the yellow daffodils that can be seen adorning the grass covered-elevation that is the tower's support were planted as a visual epitaph to the people who died during the siege, six leaves to symbolise the Star of David and an annual reminder of the need to learn from our past ignorance.

In the years following the massacre the walls of Clifford's Tower were often observed to turn red and the phenomenon became known as 'Jew's Blood'.

The York Barguest, a large, black demon hound (a story we shall be visiting imminently, see page 30) was seen at the gate of the tower in 1686 and, much more recently and far less alarmingly, members of an overnight ghost watch in 2005 observed a ghostly Red Setter in the same place.

*A*nd before we take leave of the tower we must visit the aforementioned spectral hell hound.

THE YORK BARGUEST

*A*lthough a shape-shifter by nature, the people of the north of England know the Barguest as a large, demonic, black dog with flaming eyes and razor-sharp teeth. They are common in British folklore and are known in Wales as the 'Gwyligi', or 'Dog of Darkness and in the east of England in Cambridgeshire as 'Black Shuck'.

One of these fearful creatures was said to haunt the ravine known as Trollers Gill near Appletreewick in the Yorkshire Dales. It shared its sinister territory with Scandinavian trolls, who were equally as nasty and would hurl rocks at unwary travellers.

Although its name and even its form appear to vary, one detail that the Barguest appears to have in common across Britain is that of the omen of disaster. In Jersey the 'Tchico' is a warning of an impending storm and, as with other spectral manifestations of the hellhound, it is considered a portent of death.

Its name is thought to derive from the pronunciation of the word ghost as 'guest' by the people of the north of England and the word 'burh', an Anglo-Saxon name for a town or fortress, hence 'burh-guest', or 'town-ghost'. Others think it may have a German origin in 'Berg-geist, or 'mountain demon' or possibly 'Bar-geist', meaning 'bear demon', as a result of its appearance at times as a bear.

The York Barguest is said to haunt the many alleyways and snickets that tunnel throughout the city and in 2010 was observed doggy-paddling through one of the flooded snickets, which I don't supposed did its 'terrifying demon from hell' image much good. However, it is our sincerest hope that you do not encounter the creature on your current travels.

Although not confined to a single location, the Barguest's position in the walk at this junction is attributable to a specific and recorded sighting by a guard and a subsequent further witness at the gate of Clifford's Tower on the night of 7 March 1686. The incident took place following the hanging of a local witch, a detail that may or may not be relevant and although on this occasion it chose not to appear as a dog, it instead managed to take on three entirely different and apparently unconnected forms.

Investigating a loud noise in the vicinity of the castle porch the guard was witness to a scroll appearing beneath the gate. His initial surprise become one of astonishment when the scroll transformed into a monkey. Not content with this, the Barguest changed again, this time into a turkey and, after summoning the under-keeper, both men watched as the apparition returned to its original form of a scroll and disappeared back under the gate.

DICK TURPIN'S GRAVE

Dick Turpin (see page 94), who, despite the glorification of William Harrison Ainsworth's 1834 novel *Rookwood*, was a vicious thief who's early life as an apprentice butcher was clearly insufficient to meet his needs. Finding in the notorious Essex Gang a group of people whose appalling attitude towards life and belongings matched is own he joined them in victimising farmers in a reign of terror that included not only stealing their possessions but also torturing them. When King George had decided that this must be stopped he placed a fifty pound bounty on the head of Turpin, who by now had teamed up with the highwayman 'Captain' John King and was robbing travellers from a base in Epping Forest.

With the reward for his capture as a motivation, a gamekeeper tracked them to their refuge and was duly shot by Turpin and died as a result. Not wishing to face the potential consequences of this action, Turpin fled north and adopted the name John Palmer, establishing what appears to have been a prosperous business as a horse trader, although his success was largely as a result of supplementing his stock by stealing.

This fact came to light when, for reasons that don't seem clear, Turpin shot a rooster that belonged to the landlord of the Ferry Inn in Brough in East Yorkshire.

This prompted an investigation which exposed Turpin's larceny and subsequently resulted in his incarceration for the last six months of his life in the castle prison, before being executed at Tyburn on York's Knavesmire in 1739.

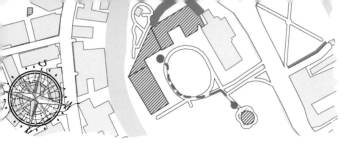

When at the foot of the tower's steps, straight ahead of you is our next haunted site.

YORK CASTLE MUSEUM

Housed in the former York Castle's debtors' and female prisons the York Castle Museum experiences ghostly disturbances that are being reported even to this day (see page 92). In addition to the large amount of history on display, including a mock up of a Victorian Street with period-costumed actors and authentic sounds, the original use of the buildings adds an historic weight and atmosphere that may account for a good many of the spectral experiences.

Its most famous inmate was the highwayman Dick Turpin (see page 31), a horse thief who fled his home county of Essex after shooting dead a gamekeeper who was attempting to capture him for the fifty pound reward money. Weird scratching, disembodied voices and the rattling of chains have all been heard by museum staff emanating from the cells.

There has also been a number of reports by visitors of an old woman dressed in black sitting by a fireplace and a number of audio based hauntings including people singing. A man dressed in black has also been witnessed and may be the ghost of a vicar and interestingly, given the proximity of the sighting of the York Barguest (see page 30), there have also been sightings of a spectral dog.

For a more detailed article on the Museum and its spectral residents, see page 92.

ST GEORGE'S FIELD

Although now independent of each other as a result of the construction of Skeldergate bridge in 1881, St Georges Field and Tower Gardens once formed an extended riverside walk created for the Georgian gentry. The north-west border of Tower Gardens is formed by a small part of the city wall that once connected Castlegate Postern with Davy Tower, now a private residence.

York's inaugural public space subsequently became popular as the ideal location for settling disputes by duel, and legend has it that the Earl of Strafford was dispatched in this manner one morning and that his staggering wraith, accompanied by a spine-chilling scream, has been witnessed by a number of hapless individuals[1].

A further sighting of the ubiquitous Dick Turpin has also been reported in this area on a number of occasions, resplendent in his tricorn hat and flowing black cape and invariably riding a horse.

RIVER OUSE

It isn't just the ancient buildings in York that house spectral forms; the Ouse, largest of the two rivers that flow through the city centre has two ghosts that have been witnessed, one as recently as 2010.

The more vintage sighting is of a phantom that wanders aimlessly around the shoreline, and it has been supposed that it is the spirit of a drowned person.

The more recent sighting is that of a person rowing a boat up the river. It was relayed to the Fringe Weird Report and therefore it must be assumed that the witness knew that it was a ghost, possibly only because it would be highly unusual to see a row boat on the modern-day Ouse.

CASTLEGATE HOUSE

Meeting place of the Alcuin Lodge of Freemasons, Castlegate House is a beautiful Georgian mansion designed by the architect John Carr and built in 1762.

Reports have made of a spectral woman who appears to glide down the staircase before vanishing in front of the astonished witnesses.

33

ST MARY'S CHURCH

St Mary's church was founded in the eleventh century although the building occupying the site now is primarily fifteenth century. It ceased to be a place of worship in 1958 and for a while was home to an exhibition entitled 'The York Story'. It is now utilised by York Museums Trust as a gallery for contemporary art exhibitions.

Although its ghost is no longer seen, he has a fascinating back story. On 23 April 1605, after descending into a pit of despair at what he perceived was a hopeless and impoverished future for himself and his family, Walter Calverley took it upon himself to put his wife and children out of his misery by murdering them[1]. He succeeded where two of his boys were concerned but his wife Philippa was spared by the strength of the whale bone in her corset. His infant third son also escaped harm by being at his wet nurse's home some twelve miles away. As Calverley galloped there to exact the fate he had planned for the unwitting child, his horse threw him and he was consequently arrested.

Somewhat reminiscent of Margaret Clitherow (see page 47) Calverley was sentenced to be crushed to death and was dispatched at York Castle by being placed underneath a board which was then loaded with weights. He was buried at St Mary's and his ghost was often seen in the churchyard, although only for a short time. This may be due to a local folktale that attests that his body was dug up shortly after and taken back to the family home in in Calverley, West Yorkshire, where a more dramatic manifestation began with Walter appearing on a horseback, his eyes glowing red[2].

BISHOPTHORPE

Bishopthorpe is a village just south of York and seems to favour headless spirits. The first sighting displays an obvious reason for this, the second is a little more obscure.

An unrecorded number of years ago the village claimed residence to an affluent woman who appears to have been murdered for her money. Presumably she lived alone as the amount of time that had passed before her body was discovered was such that decomposition had resulted in her head falling away from the neck. Subsequently her ghost, still devoid of its head, roamed the area for a number of years after her death.

And why be content with a headless woman when you can manifest a headless man accompanied by four headless horses? They used to be seen thundering along Bishopthorpe Road, the horses pulling a coach and the man dressed in black, but have not been seen for some time.

It is tempting to wonder if the coach was in fact a funeral carriage, and the spectral replay is of the poor headless woman being taken to her grave by bearers with either a macabre sense of humour or a strange idea of respectful observance.

*H*aving finished your tour of the most excellent exhibits within the museum, head back towards Clifford's Tower and take the left exit path to Tower Street. Turn right and keep an eye out on your left for a York attraction that not only boasts theatrical terror but can lay claim to bonafide ghosts too.

YORK DUNGEON

*G*iven that you are strolling around one of the most haunted cities in the world and have willingly embarked on a journey to seek out the locations that are known to have ghosts, it's a fair assumption that you like being scared. In which case, you are in the right place.

In addition to the numerous York themed horrors that are played out for the benefit of visitors to the York Dungeon there are, if you're lucky, bonus frights from the non paying visitors. Although the building is Victorian it stands on the site of what was once part of an extensive Friary that was home to the The Order of the Franciscans, also known as the Greyfriars. After three hundred years of use the Friary fell victim to Henry VIII's Dissolution of the Monasteries and all that remains is one outer wall. This, it would appear, is enough to keep three of the original residents tethered to the earthly realm as they have been seen, walking in a line, at the rear of the building. Visitors have also reported the muffled sound of voices when there has been nobody around to make any noise, and subsequently been told that the ghostly whispers are not part of any of the exhibitions. A small girl who apparently goes by the

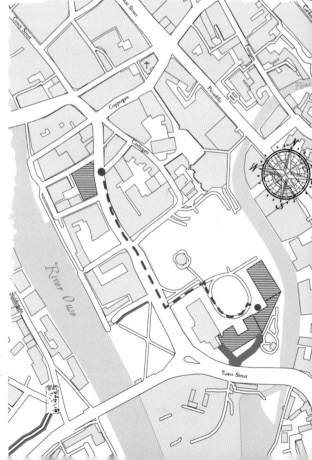

10. Castle Museum to the York Dungeon

name of Emily has been seen and may be the spook responsible for a contractor hastily exiting the building a number of years ago as a result of his ladder being inexplicably pulled out from under him. Also witnessed is an an unusually contemporary looking apparition attired in blue dungarees and a flat cap. An elderly man, it has been suggested that he may be a former caretaker.

COPPERGATE SHOPS

The Coppergate Centre was once the site for Craven's Sweet Factory, run by Mary Ann Hicks following the death of her husband Thomas Craven. In 1881 they had one hundred employees who Mary would keep a watchful eye on while perched atop a high wooden chair.

Poltergeist activity was reported even when the factory was still standing and although production moved first to Foss Islands and ultimately to Poppleton Road, resulting in the demolition of the old factory to make way for the shopping centre, employees in the new shops have stated that the ghostly activity has continued, including the wilful triggering of fire alarms.

It should be noted that when the factory site was cleared and the foundations were being dug for the new shops, a wealth of Viking material, including timber from buildings, was uncovered. The excavation led to the birth of the Jorvik Viking Centre where many of the artefacts are on display.

Perhaps it wasn't just the earthly Viking remains that were disturbed, but something a little more sinister.

11. York Dungeon to Priory Church of the Holy Trinity

If you decide to be brave and enter the York Dungeon your exit will be around the side of the building in Cumberland Street, in which case you will have to walk back to the entrance at the front. Once there, or if you're still there having decided to postpone (or chicken out) of your visit to the Dungeon, turn left (although not immediate left or you'll end up heading down Cumberland Street) and walk up Clifford Street until you get to the end. At the junction, turn left and walk over the bridge until you reach the bottom of a cobbled hill. This is Micklegate and the location of two of our haunted locations, one of them being Micklegate Bar at the top. Walk about two hundred yards up the hill and you will see to your left a large church raised and set back from the street. This is the eerie aspect of the first of our two stops.

PRIORY CHURCH OF THE HOLY TRINITY

Built on the grounds of a Benedictine priory church that is listed in the Domesday Book of 1086 as one of five great northern churches, the Holy Trinity (not to be confused with the Holy Trinity church that we will be visiting later) is in possession of a curious haunting that involves three separate entities. Clothed in white, there are two woman and a child whose sightings have resulted in two variations as to their origins. Some believe that the three are connected, with one of the woman being the mother of the child and the second woman being the child's nanny. Documented by the Reverend S. Baring Gould in his book *Yorkshire Oddities* the young mother, her face obscured by a veil, would often appear during daylight hours. She would then be joined by the second female, described as a nursemaid, who would be accompanied by a small child. The spectres' origin was said to be that of an ill-fated family that lived close to the church. The father died and was buried in the churchyard close to the east window. Shortly after, the child fell victim to the plague which, due to plague regulations, resulted in him being buried outside the city walls. Grief stricken with loss the mother also died relatively soon after and was buried with her husband in the church grounds. The ghostly re-enactment is the mother's continued attempt to re-unite herself with her lost child.

It appears that the re-building of the chancel in 1886 ended the sightings and no further reports have been made since the 1890s.

The second theory is that it is only the mother and child that are united in their somewhat doomed undertaking and that the second woman is not in any way connected other than by roaming the same location in an equally ineffective manner.

Her story has it that she was the abbess at the time of the reformation and lost her life in a futile attempt to protect the church from Henry VIII's invading men.

The confusion may lie in the very close similarity of the names of this church and the aforementioned Holy Trinity on Goodramgate. Lewis Spence's *An Encyclopaedia of Occultism*, published in 1920, relates a vivid and highly detailed version of the abbess story but links it to the sightings of the ghostly nun seen at the church in Goodramgate.[1]

*T*urning left out of the church will take you further up Micklegate until you get to the top of the hill where, certainly from an historic perspective, the most important of York's four gateways will tower above you.

MICKLEGATE BAR

*F*or those travelling North to York in the twelfth century, Micklegate Bar would be the primary access to the city, and given that anybody of any importance in those days invariably came from the south, Micklegate Bar became something of a focal point for the celebration of visits from eminent individuals. A number of reigning monarchs have graced the Bar with their presence and have obligingly indulged in the tradition of requesting entry from the Lord Mayor.

Up until 1754 a notably gruesome aspect of the Bar was the authorities' inclination for exhibiting the severed heads of people who had run foul of them above the gate. Not the warmest of welcomes and one can only hope they were (at least temporarily) removed before the arrival of any visiting sovereign.

As with the York Dungeon, the resident spectre is that of a small girl, although this one is known by the name of Sarah Brocklebank. Often seen walking the passageways of the Bar her presence is associated with the noise of keys being rattled, sometimes when she is visible but also as a disembodied clamour. In life, she was the daughter of the resident bar keeper, whose responsibility for the keys was clearly one of great importance; it would be rather awkward if the king was left at the gate because someone had lost the key. Sadly for the unfortunate Sarah, this is precisely what she managed to do and spent the entirety of her life attempting to locate them. She has also been seen running up Stonegate towards the Mansion House, the residence of the Lord Mayor. It is thought that she may have realised where she had left the keys and is repeatedly hurrying to inform everyone. Presumably a replacement lock was fitted to the gate but the mortified Sarah was apparently so obsessed with her quest that she continued her search until she eventually found them, at which point she promptly died.

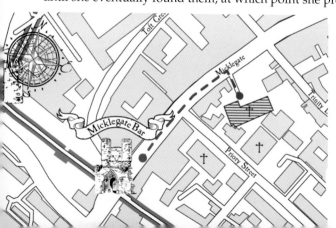

12. Priory Church of the Holy Trinity to Micklegate Bar

BAR CONVENT

Founded in 1686 the Bar Convent is the longest established convent in England, the resident nuns belonging to the Congregation of Jesus.

The current building, constructed in the 1760s when Catholic worship was still illegal, has a hidden chapel with eight exists and a priest hole in preparation for the inevitable raids by the authorities.

Not that it was only the magistrates they needed to fear. In 1696 the original building was set upon by a frenzied mob who were only prevented from doing harm to the sisters by the apparent materialisation of St Michael astride a horse. A commemorative engraving graces the area above the front door and further details of the convent's history can be studied within its own museum on the site,

Also available to be viewed is the surviving hand of Margaret Clitherow (see page 50)[1].

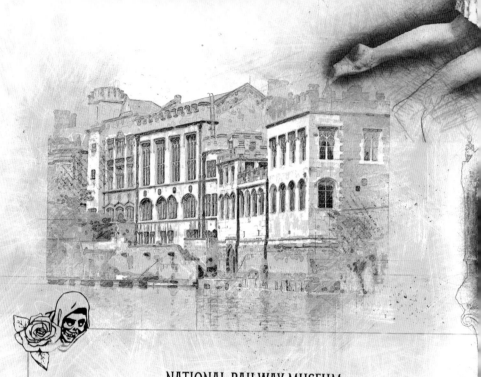

NATIONAL RAILWAY MUSEUM

For those of you with an additional interest in locomotives a visit to the National Railway Museum is an opportunity to indulge in two interests for the price of one; not that it will actually cost you anything as the museum is free.

A number of people have reported a strong feeling of being watched when viewing one of the old sleeper carriages and in 2008 a ghost hunting team presenting a live show after the museum was closed witnessed a figure walking up one of the royal carriages. A member of staff informed them that this had been experienced a number of times.

In 2013 an Interpretation Developer in the Public Programmes team posted three photographs purporting to be of ghosts that had been taken in the museum. One clearly shows a man dressed in what could be period clothing either entering or exiting a steam train cab in the museum's south yard[1].

Now we head back over to the other side of the river taking the scenic route. Facing Micklegate Bar you will see to your right a set of steps that will take you up on to the medieval wall. At the top of the first flight of steps you can either turn left and pay a visit to the Henry VII Experience or save that pleasure for another time and turn right and ascend the second flight of steps and head west along the city wall. This section of the wall ends at the southern end of Lendal Bridge where you should turn left onto the bridge and walk about hundred yards. Cross over over the road (take care, it's a busy one) and you should see a turning right into the street known as Lendal. Walk to the end of Lendal and as you emerge into St Helen's Square the previously mentioned Mansion House (see page 40) will be to your right (if Sarah is around she'll be running toward you from the left). To the right of this is the entranceway to our next haunted establishment.

GUILDHALL

Built for the Guild of St Christopher and St George the Guildhall has been used for city authority meetings for hundreds of years and the York City Council still have their full meetings in the council chambers today.

It has also been used for a number of additional purposes, notably the trial and conviction of Margaret Clitherow (see page 50) in 1586.

The fifteenth-century building that hides behind the Mansion House was built on the site of an older meeting place known as Common Hall, and the remains of Common Hall Lane are part of the Guildhall basement. The lane is haunted (see page 104) with spectral figures and the main part of the building has a number of reported poltergeist phenomena, including slamming doors, footsteps and eerie voices emanating from nowhere. Particularly uncanny was the discovery by staff of a footprint that was small enough to be attributed to a child. Not in itself a great deal of cause for alarm but for the fact that it was found on top of a grandfather clock.

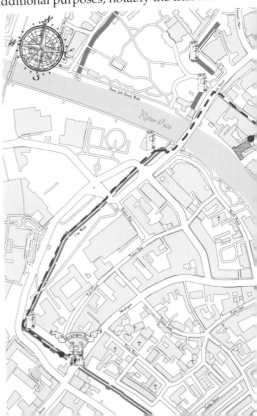

13. Micklegate Bar to the Guildhall

*O*nce back at the entrance, beneath which are the remains of the Roman road that ran from the river to the Minster, turn right and continue up Coney Street for about a hundred yards and our next ghostly location will be visible on the left through a small archway in between two shops.

JUDGE'S COURT

*O*ne of the many buildings in York that would retain almost complete anonymity were it not for useful books such as this guiding you to them.[1] Hidden from the bustle of Coney Street, Judge's Court is a four-storey Georgian building that was in use between 1720 and 1806[2] as a lodging house for judges, hence its name. The judges would visit York on a twice yearly basis for the purpose of presiding over trials on criminals incarcerated at York Castle, including the notorious highwayman Dick Turpin, who pops up with alarming frequency in ghost related matters (see page 31) and who was sentenced to hang in 1739 by Judge William Chapple.

The connection with Turpin may account for the nature of the haunting. The phantom has been described as a man dressed in black (and we doubt that it's Jonny Cash) whose appearances, in a strange echo of the ghost that occupies the location we have just come from, are accompanied by a jangling noise. However, in this case it is not keys that are responsible, for the source of the noise is a broken spur.

It would be a reasonable conjecture that perhaps Dick Turpin's restless spirit, vexed at the impudence of a man condemning him to be hanged for the trifling misdeed of horse theft and murder, has chosen to wander the building where the impertinent gentleman laid his head the day before the sentencing. However, a sinister discovery some years following the initial manifestations may well have provided an eerie corroboration for the sightings and also an alternative proposition as to the origin of the ghost. The remains of a large man were found in a well nearby, along with the remnants of his riding

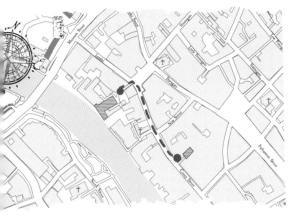

boots. Attached to the boots were a pair of spurs. one of which was clearly broken. This unfortunate man seems far more likely to be the source of the haunting, and it can't be Dick Turpin as he's buried elsewhere in York (see page 31).

14. Guildhall to Judge's Court

ST CRUX CHURCH

The original St Crux was listed in the Domesday Book and so existed in the eleventh century, at that time owned by the Count of Mortain. In the early twelfth century ownership had passed into the hands of St Mary's Abbey (see page 58) and it was re-built in the early part of the fifteenth century. Post Dissolution of the Monasteries it was then in the hands of the Crown, and a new tower was added at the end of the seventeenth century.

Finally falling within the control of the archbishop in 1868 the church was once an imposing sight with its grand, Italian-style tower, and was considered a thing of beauty in its early years, with Francis Drake noting in 1736 that the tower was 'a handsome new steeple of brick coined with stone'. However, its visual popularity did not endure and when the tower became unstable and parts of it began dropping off (including four urns that once graced the tower's upper part) funds to restore it did not materialise and it was demolished in 1887, the only residue of its former existence being the small parish hall built in its place.

Stonework from the church was recycled in the building of the hall and about five feet of the original north wall still remains, adjoined to number 23 Shambles. Monuments from the original church have been placed within the hall and the window in the east wall is the church's south aisle window.

45

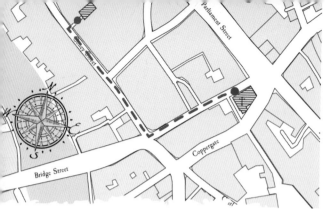

merging from the tunnel that leads you back out, turn left and continue along Coney Street. Take the first left into Market Street and up ahead you'll see a fork in the street. Just before it to your right is the entrance to a small street named Peter Lane. Enter the lane and at the top, turn left and enter the alleyway that will take you onto High Ousegate. Turn left and you'll see the church that is our next ghostly destination ahead of you on the right.

ALL SAINTS' CHURCH

lthough not the edifice that is in front of you today, there has been a church on this site prior to the Norman Conquest in the eleventh-century and the first documented allusion to the church is in the Domesday Book of 1086. If that were not old enough, folklore attests to a church being built here for St Cuthbert in 685, presumably to coincide with his consecration as Bishop of Lindisfarne.

The Guild Church of York that stands today was built in the fourteenth century and contains a marvellous fifteenth century addition in the form of a lantern tower that was built to guide travellers to the city through the Forest of Galtres to the north.[1]

Unlike the roguish countenance of our previous phantom the ghost at All Saints is know to be a beautiful woman in white with long hair. She apparently appears to be entirely real and makes her appearances at funeral services, gently welcoming the mourners to the church before disappearing.

If you exit through the north entrance you can have a look at the rather weird re-creation of a twelfth-century door knocker depicting the mouth to hell.

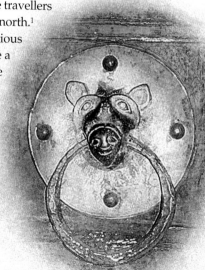

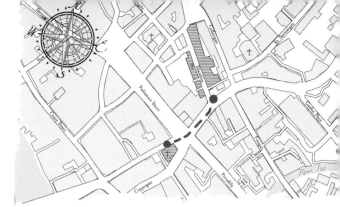

urn right and walk straight ahead so that you're on the left hand side of the road named Pavement and you'll see a church hall ahead. This is at the foot of our next haunted location and one of the most famous streets in Britain.

SHAMBLES

nternationally Shambles is possibly the best known street in York and is certainly one of the most atmospheric. In medieval times Shambles was also the name given to the area, which contained a whole network of lanes and alleys with the Shambles itself being home to the city's butchers. The buildings that lined these streets and formed the walls of the alleyways are long gone, as are all the butchers, but Shambles is still very much alive and well, hosting primarily tourist-themed shops but still proudly displaying its heritage with many of the shops still sporting the Shamels, or benches, that gave the street its name.

Before embarking on your journey up Shambles you will see to your right, on the corner of Pavement, the site of the St Crux (Holy Cross) church. Having fallen into disrepair and become unsafe the church was demolished in 1887, but not before a number of spectres had become associated with the building. A number of people saw a man standing within the church and looking out at the street. As he tended to appear very early in the morning and never made any attempt to come out of the church (and no one dared go in) it was assumed he was a ghost.

Prior to the Second World War there were further reports of a gentleman who may be the same apparition, although this ghost appears to have been witnessed either out in the street or through a window. Elegantly dressed and impeccably well mannered he would cheerily acknowledge passers by with a smile or wave and ladies would be regaled with a doff of his bowler hat. One particular woman stated that she had seen this man on a regular basis for years. She remembered him from her teenage years and he was still present when she was in her forties. However, plucking up the courage on one occasion to speak to him, he vanished.

In addition to the two gentleman was a lady, apparently dressed in white, who would follow the York waits, a group of watchmen whose duties also included the provision of music for the general populace and would do so by roaming the streets kitted out in colourful attire and silver badges. The lady in white would emerge, somewhat alarmingly, from the St Crux churchyard and follow at a respectful distance, clearly enjoying the music, but would not answer to any of the calls made to her by the musicians. She would remain with them until they entered Goodramgate, at which point she would vanish.

A third haunting was experienced by a policeman in the early part of the twentieth century when his rounds took him late one night past the front of the church. As he walked towards Shambles he was struck by the eerie sound of a funeral march emanating from within the church, which was clearly strange considering the lateness of the hour. While standing and listening, the doors of the church swung open and the noise of a procession joined that of the organ music

DAVYGATE

Despite its rather contemporary sounding name, archaeological excavations have revealed a history to this part of York that dates back to the late Iron Age[1].

The street itself is of medieval origin and takes its name from its most important building; Davy Hall (also known as Lardiner Hall). This was the seat of administration for the Forest of Galtres (see page 46), and also its court and prison, the inmates of which were mostly poachers. Its resident governor in the early twelfth century was David, named Le Lardiner after his role as crown-appointed steward of the larder that stored the venison and domestic meat produce originating from the forest, and who inherited both position and title from his great grandfather John, who had arrived here with William the Conqueror.

The Hall is long gone, as are the Romans that occupied Davygate over a thousand years earlier but in 1958 two woman who were strolling along the street suddenly found themselves in the midst of a great battle. Fighting all around them were Roman troops and opponents who they described as Barbarians, so possibly the Brigantes, a Celtic tribe who occupied the north of England before the Roman invasion.

In a fabulously prosaic culmination to this experience, the scene vanished when a van drove past.

and, although he could see no one, he felt the brush of their clothes against his legs as they passed by. Once the noise of their movement had died away, the church doors swung shut and all became silent.

About half way up the Shambles is the shrine to St Margaret Clitherow, martyred in the tollbooth of the original Ouse Bridge in 1586 for the crime of harbouring Catholic priests. After a number of imprisonments her home in the Shambles was raided and although the concealed clergyman managed to escape, Margaret was arrested, tried and sentenced to death by the rather barbaric practice of being crushed to death. Pleas for her pregnancy to be taken into account and a more lenient approach fell on deaf ears and she was stripped naked, laid on her back and a stone placed beneath her back. Her own front door was then placed on top of her and a sufficient number of additional stones were then piled on top of the door to break her back. Despite the traumatic nature of her death, many people have reported an uncanny sense of peace and calm within the shrine, despite the level of noise and people just outside it. A gentleman also claimed to have witnessed the ghost of Margaret Clitherow one morning while walking down Shambles on route to buy a newspaper.[1]

More recent ghostly experiences have included the sighting of a man sitting in the corner of the Earl Grey Tea Rooms who does not appear to be real, and the same establishment has generated a report of a child's hand grasping a customer while she was in the ladies' toilet. When turning around, there was nobody there.

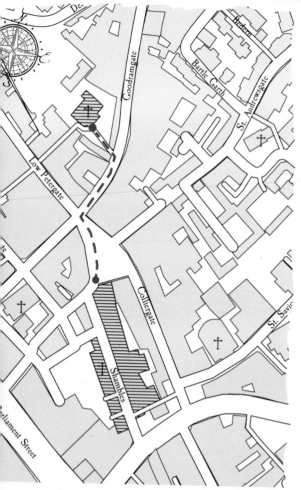

17. Shambles to Holy Trinity Church

ou may be some time taking in the quaint atmosphere and charm of Shambles but once you have reached the top you will see King's Square to your right. Follow the path around the square to the left and when you're at the crossroads of Petergate turn right into Goodramgate. Walk along for about a hundred yards and keep your eyes trained to the left where you will see an arch with an iron railing gate. This is the entrance to a fabulously old and peaceful part of York that, if you're not careful, is easy to miss. Plus, it has ghosts.

HOLY TRINITY CHURCH

n the heart of York lies an oasis of tranquility that processes a peace and calm that belies its turbulent historical connections. With York Minster towering behind it, two very different apparitions are said to haunt this fifteenth century church and the first, Sir Thomas Percy, the 7th Earl of Northumberland and lover of Anne Boleyn before her marriage to Henry VIII, was beheaded for treason.

Like his namesake father before him, who was executed at Tyburn for his part in the uprising against Henry VIII following the dissolution of some of the smaller monasteries, Sir Thomas conspired against Queen Elizabeth I with the intention of freeing the imprisoned Mary Queen of Scots and re-establishing the Catholic faith that was being eroded by the Protestant monarchy. However, their plot was exposed to the Queen which prompted the leaders to assemble their forces at Durham where they headed south via Staindrop, Darlington, Richmond, and Ripon, restoring the ancient service in each place. At Ripon they defeated the forces of Sir William Ingleby and marched on to Knaresborough, Wetherby, Clifford Moor and their final victory at Barnard Castle. Their next destination was York.

Unfortunately, a 5000 strong defence was waiting for them. The uprising dissipated and the leaders fled to Scotland. Thomas was betrayed by the Earl of Moreton, Viceroy of Scotland and was taken to York and beheaded in Pavement, his head being stuck on a spike and displayed at Micklegate Bar. Eventually it was buried in the graveyard at Holy Trinity and the Earl's headless torso has been witnessed on many occasions wandering around the grave stones in an endless quest to be re united with his lost head.

A plaque affixed to the wall almost directly opposite the entrance to the snicket 'Lady Peckett's Yard' (see page 75) marks the sigte of the execution.

A second ghost in the form of a nun has also been reported. She appears on winter evenings and walks the church and grounds reciting the Lord's Prayer and has occasionally been confused with the ghost that appears in the Priory Church of the Holy Trinity on Micklegate (see page 38).

LUND'S COURT - FORMERLY MAD ALICE LANE

The Mad Alice of today is actually Alicia Stabler, who runs extremely good guided tours around York's bloodier (historically anyway) locations and will gleefully inform you of all the nasty aspects that make up its history.

The Mad Alice that gave the snicket known as Lund's Court its original name is something more of an enigma. The lane that connects Low Petergate with Swinegate was undoubtedly named Mad Alice and there must be a reason for that. Unfortunately nobody seems to no what the reason is, although according to popular folktale the woman was a resident of the lane (presumably another, preceding name was in existence at that point) named Alice Smith and that she was hanged in 1825 in the St Michael le Belfrey church (or it may have been York Castle) for no other crime than that of being insane. An alternative version of the story is that she had been abused by her husband to such an extent that she murdered him with poison, and that her subsequent hanging was the punishment for her crime.

The conundrum is that there is no record of an Alice Smith being hung in York, either in that year or any other year, which suggests (discounting theories of a cover up) that the story is complete fiction.

In which case the question is: who was Mad Alice and why did they name a street after her?

*W*hen leaving the church, rather than go back the way you came in, turn to your right and walk around the side of the church and you will see an alternative exit that will bring you out onto Petergate. Turn right and you'll see the Minster dominating the end of the street. Walk towards and the second turn on the left is our next ghost infused location.

STONEGATE

*S*tonegate is a two thousand year old street that has been witness to every piece of York's varied and turbulent history. The Romans established the road and the Via Praetoria that ran from the fortress on the site of the Minster to the bridge on the river Ouse is still there, about 6 feet below.

According to Francis Drake it acquired its name as a result of the vast quantity of limestone that was hauled up it from the river to build the Minster but however it was named there is no denying that it has plenty of ghosts.

We're entering from the top of the street so we'll work down the numbers, beginning with one of the more famous of York's ghost stories at No 41. Now an Antiques Centre, this remarkably tall and thin building is host to the ghost of a six-year-old Victorian girl who tragically fell to her death by toppling over the bannister of the staircase that runs up through the centre of the building. She has been seen on a number of occasions over the years, including sitting on top of the shop counter and she can also be heard walking the stairs. Even when she can't be seen, she makes her presence known by moving stock around.

18. Holy Trinity Church to Stonegate

53

A little further on is No. 35, which for a period of two hundred years served as the home of publishers The Sign of the Bible and was occupied from 1757 by John Hinxman, notable for publishing *The Life and Opinions of Tristram Shandy, Gentleman,* the famous work by York's own Laurence Sterne (see page 99).

Now notorious for being the most haunted building in York and also the scene of celebrity ghost hunter Derek Acorah's throttling experience. His explanation for being dragged back by the throat and pushed up against the panelled wall came from his spirit guide Sam, who explained that an extremely annoyed man, apparently aged about forty, was decidedly unhappy about the Ghost Town TV show's presence in his room and was clearly anxious for them to leave.

This was in 2006 when the building was owned by astrologer Jonathan Cainer, who'd purchased it in 1999 and began the task of some much needed renovation. He stated in an interview at the time that he was aware of a few ghosts but that the work being undertaken had stirred up a considerable increase in spectral activity and that the property was now "… like Piccadilly Circus."

From 2007 the volume of ghosts was made available to the general public when the spook-infested building was opened up to the public as a ghost attraction. Aptly named 'Haunted', it sadly closed in 2014 but during its existence as an open house for both serious and casual ghost hunters it proved extremely popular and resulted in endless sightings.

The mediaeval building that stands there today was built in 1482, but there are records showing that a property has existed on the site for over a thousand years. Small wonder that there are so many ghosts inhabiting it, including a distressed woman in the kitchen and a man identified by the medium Ian Doherty as Tom, who dresses in black, wears a hat and seems to favour the wood-panelled room bedecked with carvings of flowers and demons. Although this is the very location of Mr Acorah's rather unfortunate incident there seems to be no suggestion that his assailant and Tom are the same entity.

Few haunted locations in York seem to be without a spectral monk and 35 Stonegate is no exception, the balding chap having been seen in one of the upstairs rooms. Meanwhile, a sophisticated looking woman attired in Georgian clothing has also been witnessed and many reports have been made by people who have had parts of their body clasped by an invisible hand. A member of staff during its time as Haunted was about to evict a child from the building after closing hours when it rounded a corner and disappeared.

A number of poltergeist manifestations have been reported, including the opening and closing of doors, scratching sounds emanating from the attic and the inevitable sounds of creaking floorboards, despite the recipients of these ghostly noises being alone in the property.

Further down, on the opposite side of the street, is 18-20, where a young woman was disturbed in the changing rooms when she saw a girl standing behind her in the mirror, When she turned to confront her the girl made a hasty exit through the wall. It transpired that there had once been a door where the girl had vanished.

A perhaps welcome break from the overcrowded street of Stonegate (it tends to be busy with people as well) will see us stroll to our next destination via the charming ambience of the Museum Gardens. Indeed, it is the museum itself that we will be visiting.

urn right at the bottom of Stonegate and walk up Blake Street, perhaps stopping for a brief perusal of the delights on offer in The Imaginarium and then turn left into Museum Street. Before long you will see the entrance to the gardens on the opposite side of the road. Follow the path from the gate and stay to the right of the fork and the museum will present itself to you.

YORKSHIRE MUSEUM

s with the Holy Trinity Church, the Yorkshire Museum's setting is not suggestive of any dark, unnatural events. Set in ten acres of beautiful botanical gardens the site is also home to the remains of St Mary's Abbey, itself haunted (see page 58), along with a fourteenth century Hospitium and also part

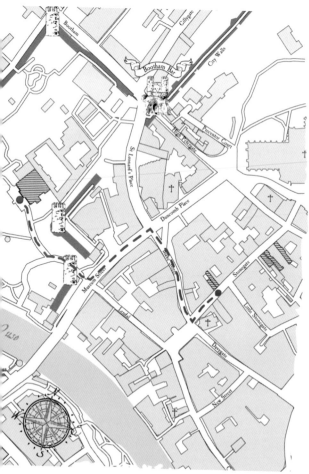

of a Roman fortress wall. However, George Thomas, the caretaker of the museum at the time, suffered an an early evening encounter that became so notorious that none other than the Society for Psychical Research became involved in the investigation.

The year was 1950 when the otherwise unremarkable Mr Thomas noticed a man dressed in a frock coat reading a book in the museum library. He assumed that the gentleman was a visitor that had become so engrossed in his research that he was unaware of the fact that it was closing time. As he approached the man he realised that he was very agitated and was muttering "I must find it". At

19. Stonegate to the Yorkshire Museum

this point the figure vanished, dropping the book to the floor.

Having mentioned the incident to a few others a small group gathered one night in the hope that the spectre would re-appear. Although they were to be disappointed by a lack of manifestation they were rewarded by the startling display of a book flying from its shelf and hurtling to the floor with a loud thud. There was also a noticeable drop in the temperature at around the time of this occurrence,  something that was in keeping with previous reports of 'an intense cold' by members of the museum staff. Having recovered themselves the book was examined and found to be the very same book that had fallen from the hands of the disappearing spook witnessed by George Thomas. The book, *Antiquities and Curiosities of the Church* had been donated to the museum by Alderman Edward Wooler, a photograph of whom was shown to Mr Thomas who identified it as the ghost he had seen in the library.

Despite there being no more reported sightings of Alderman Wooler the book was seen to remove itself from shelves and drop to the floor on a number of further occasions by staff at the museum and, although it is not known what the man was so anxious to locate, there is a brown stain on the inside cover that may once have had a photograph or document attached to it.

The book was subsequently moved to the City Library where it seemed to be much more settled and all gravity-defying acts came to an end. Perhaps, like so many ghosts who seem to be confined to a particular building or place, Alderman Wooler is unable to leave the Yorkshire Museum, in which case, having been separated from the book, he is doomed never to find the item that he was so desperately searching for.

A further book-related sighting has been reported although on this occasion the manifestation took place in the Tempest Anderson Hall, built in 1912 and used as the museum's auditorium. The witness clearly saw a man garbed in a Victorian outfit reaching to retrieve a book from a shelf near the stage. Upon turning towards the witness the ghost revealed itself to possess a face completely free of features.

ST MARY'S ABBEY

The original abbey church dates back to 1055 when it was dedicated to the Norwegian King Olaf who had been posthumously canonised a year after his death in 1030.

Following William the Conqueror's Harrying of the North in 1069 the abbey was given to Alan Rufus who in turn passed the lands on to Abbot Stephen of Whitby. A new Norman church was then dedicated to the Virgin Mary.

The wealthiest abbey in the north of England it occupied a large area that took in the grounds of what is now the Museum Gardens and also the site of the King's Manor, at that time the abbot's house. All that remains today are the ruins of the abbey church, rebuilt after a fire in the late thirteenth century, the Hospitium and the Wast Gate.

A monk has been seen roaming the ruins of the church and the sounds of money being counted and then dropped into a metal box have been heard and he is likely to be the same phantom that has been seen in the King's Manor.

*E*xiting from the museum, turn left and immediately left again and follow the small path that will take you to the right of a stone building, through the green gate and and at its conclusion, to your left, will be the entrance to our next haunted location, a collection of buildings steeped in ancient history.

KING'S MANOR

*K*ing's Manor appears to have one of the highest levels of spectral activity of all York's ancient buildings and for one that has been so involved in the city's history, it seems fitting that the ghostly relics are of some of its most notable inhabitants.

20. Yorkshire Museum to The King's Manor

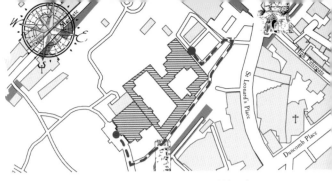

Built around 1270 to serve as the Abbot's Residence of St Mary's Abbey, its most veteran occupant is a black-hooded monk who has been sighted in various places around the Manor and may well be the same gentleman spotted walking around the ruins of the Abbey (see page 58).

With the continually impactful abolition of the monasteries by Henry VIII in 1536, the Manor became the seat of the Council of the North and subsequently the official residence of the President of the Council in 1561. The Earl of Huntingdon, who was President between 1572 and 1595, oversaw a great deal of building and extension work that included dressed stonework blocks, known as ashlar, using stone from St Mary's Abbey. Perhaps our hooded monk is keeping an eye on it.

Keeping him company is the ghost of Queen Catherine Howard, who, along with her husband Henry VIII, were guests at the manor in 1541. Catherine was only eighteen when the fifty-year-old Henry took her as his fifth wife and it is perhaps not surprising that very soon after the wedding she entered into affairs with two much younger men. One of these, Thomas Culpepper, indulged in clandestine meetings with the Queen during her stay at the Manor and perhaps it was this happy, although fatally dangerous, period that keeps her spectral presence in residence. An interesting detail of her sighting, most notably by a domestic, who was greeted by the sight of the Queen attired in a flowing green Tudor dress and walking at her through a cupboard, is that she appears to be carrying what at first were thought to be ribbons. After a number of further sightings by the maid, she realised that they were not ribbons but a bunch of roses. Catherine was sometimes known by the King's reference to her as 'the rose without a thorn' and it was later discovered by folklorist John Mitchell that a rose garden had once existed in the opposite direction to the route of the ghost. Shortly after her stay at the Manor her adultery was discovered and her young lover was hung, drawn and quartered. She herself was arrested and taken to the Tower of London by barge where she she was forced to endure the spectacle of her two lover's heads sitting atop spikes above Tower Bridge. Within a few weeks she was beheaded on Tower Green for treason.

As if by way of solidarity there is the ghost of Thomas Wentworth, President of the Council and Earl of Strafford who also fell foul of an angry King when Charles I signed his death warrant by consenting to a Bill of Attainder. Once part of English common law, the bill effectively gave the right of the King or Queen to find somebody guilty, usually of treason, without a trial. Like the Queen before him, Thomas was removed to the Tower in 1641 and subsequently beheaded. He was witnessed by an employee of the Manor who recognised him from a portrait that hung in the same room. The incident so disturbed the man that he died later that night.

Within just a few years of the untimely dispatch of Thomas Wentworth the King's Manor was able to add to its collection of spectral residents when it was besieged by Roundheads during the English Civil War. The wailing of the dying following the unsuccessful attempt to take the Manor on Trinity Sunday in 1644 can still be heard emanating from the passage leading away from the inner courtyard.

With the advent of the Stuart dynasty in 1603 Britain became a United Kingdom and the Manor played its part in a flourishing Court culture that saw regular visits from royalty throughout the period and a new building added to the Manor's existing layout. A modest period of poltergeist activity was witnessed by a teacher staying at the Manor during the years when it was home to the Yorkshire School for the Blind from 1833 until 1956. A cupboard set into the wall would be mysteriously opened as if by some unseen hand but, oddly, this only happened on occasions when she placed a particular scarf within it, a scarf of Royal Stuart Tartan.

A further Stuart connection comes from reports of a Stuart nobleman being seen and the subsequent witness by four teachers who were determined to verify his existence one Halloween. They saw the lower half of the body as the ghost descended the stairs, resplendent in appropriate Stuart period attire, but were foiled in their attempt to see more when the headmaster of the school appeared and told them all to go to bed, at which point the ghost vanished.

21. King's Manor to the Theatre Royal

Exiting the King's Manor gate, turn right and on the opposite side of the busy road that is St Leonard's Place you will see our penultimate haunted establishment.

YORK THEATRE ROYAL

There are a number of 'Grey Ladies' dotted around the more spooky parts of York (notably The York Arms and The Starre Inn public houses) but perhaps the most often seen is the hooded figure that portents a successful show at the Theatre Royal.

Founded in 1744 the theatre was built on the ruins of St Leonard's Hospital, which in the 12th century was the largest mediaeval hospital in Europe. Parts of the old crypt can still be seen in the Keregan Room and, even older, are the remains of a Roman well beneath the stage.

The sad lady that has so often been seen by performers is believed to have been a young apprentice nun working in the hospice. Having committed the dreadful sin of falling in love with a nobleman she was punished by being bricked up alive in a small room adjacent to the dress circle. Subsequently used as a dressing room, her presence has often been felt by occupants who have described a feeling of being watched and also a cold, lingering atmosphere.

However, a recent investigation by a group of psychic researchers uncovered some very different information, including the woman's name. Although it was confirmed that the lady was a nun, the reason for her internment, which was in a cell not a brick-sealed chamber, was for claiming to have seen angels at mass. Accused of possessing a "black and lying tongue", 'Therese' was threatened with harsher punishment if she didn't stay put. Despite the many alterations that have been made to the building over the years, no body has ever been found, which would suggest that the story of Therese is perhaps more accurate.

A second ghost, that of an actor, has been seen on occasion and was first witnessed on the day of his death, apparently as a result of a duel in Blake Street. The rest of the cast decided that, despite the tragedy, the show must go on and were horrified to see their former leading man stumbling around in the wings during the evening's performance.

Seemingly unrelated to either the Grey Lady or the duelling actor is the report in the 1930s of organ music being played in the theatre in the middle of the night. First heard at twenty past two it was repeated an hour later, at which point the spectral performer's obvious swan song was over, as it was never heard again.

CLIFTON LODGE

A large Victorian property it was the final residence of Joseph Rowntree, who moved into the property in 1905 and remained there until his death in 1925.

There is a legend of a resident ghost that is the spirit of a former servant. Having been made pregnant out of wedlock the humiliation drove her to murder the child, a misdeed that has tethered her to the mortal realm.

ST MICHAEL LE BELFREY

As appears quite common in York, the site of St Michael le Belfrey has been host to a church as far back as the eighth century but the present church was built more recently, in the early sixteenth century.

Although not notable for residual spooks, it was the church in which York-born Guido Fawkes was baptised in 1520 (see page 85) and was also, according to local folktale, the location of Mad Alice's execution (see page 52).

*22. Theatre Royal
to York Minster*

L eaving the theatre, turn left and continue along St Leonard's Place and turn left into Dun-combe Place where you will see our final haunted edifice (hopefully with no scaffolding) majestically reaching for the sky before you.

THE MINSTER

T owering above the centre of York, the Minster is the largest gothic cathedral in Europe, although the original Minster, founded by St Paulinus in 627 AD and built on the site of the abandoned Roman fortress, would have been a small wooden structure.[1]

Begun in 1220 by Archbishop Walter de Grey, the imposing edifice that is there today took over 250 years to complete and is the site of one of the most intriguing of York's ghost stories.

It was recorded in a book published in the middle part of the last century that a father and his two daughters, whose names were changed to protect the privacy of the family, were being accompanied by an unnamed gentleman and a number of other friends on a trip to the Minster. During the course of admiring the vast interior of the building the gentleman was rather taken aback when a man in a naval uniform came walking towards them. As York is some distance from the sea this was a rather unusual sight and he took it upon himself to draw the attention of the father's eldest daughter to the fast approaching naval officer. Instead of mild curiosity, the woman appeared intently distressed by the sight of the man and visibly paled. The gentleman called over to the father and younger daughter for some assistance but by this time the sailor was standing directly in front of them. He leaned over to the woman and whispered a most perplexing statement: "There is a future state", before moving off down the aisle.

Leaving the woman in the care of her father and sister the gentleman went after the man who had caused her such distress but failed to see or hear any sign of him. Upon his return the now recovered daughter assured her father and sister that she would be fine and that they should leave her in the charge of the gentleman. When they had moved away she explained that the man they had seen was her brother and that she knew that he must have died at sea. Her discretion was the result of not wishing her father to know such upsetting news and also the fear that she would not be believed even if she had told him. She went on to explain that many years before she and her brother had made an agreement that whichever one of them died first should, if possible, contact the other at the moment of their death.

In time, the truth of her story was borne out by the arrival of the news of her brother's death at sea, the date and time coinciding exactly with their encounter in the Minster.

In addition, the death at the inaugural stages of the eighteenth century has not prevented a man named Dean Gale attending services, and he has occasionally been seen seated in one of the pews.

That particular phantom appears to have made a once-only appearance, whereas conversely there are a number of ghosts that seem to make themselves known with alarming frequency. A ghostly hound by the name of Seamus can sometimes be heard barking at night, the result of being bricked up in one of the Minster's walls by some heartless stonemasons during its construction.

Quite recently and somewhat intriguingly a man was seen riding around York Minster on a bicycle. Given the close proximity of the York Arms pub (see page 87), its spectral cyclist may well be the same spirit.

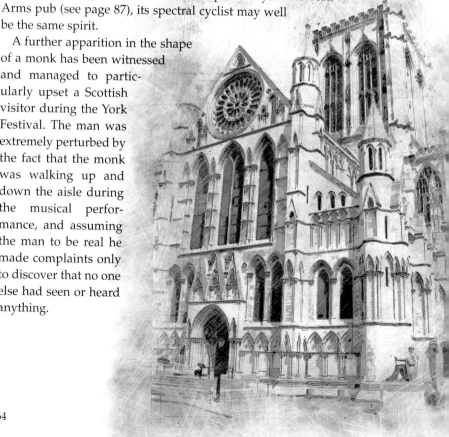

A further apparition in the shape of a monk has been witnessed and managed to particularly upset a Scottish visitor during the York Festival. The man was extremely perturbed by the fact that the monk was walking up and down the aisle during the musical performance, and assuming the man to be real he made complaints only to discover that no one else had seen or heard anything.

HAUNTED TAVERNS

Where to Begin ...

In addition to the apparently vast number of ghosts in York there are an equally large number of public houses. By no means mutually exclusive, it is entirely possible that one fact may go a long way toward accounting for the other, hence our round up of the most prominent haunted taverns in the city centre.

Although we shall assume that you may wish to partake of a beverage in each of the fine hostelries you will encounter on the walk, we are aware that there are quite a number and that this would almost certainly result in a walk rapidly becoming a stagger and subsequently petering out in an unseemly halt. As such, feel free to embark on the walk on a number of different occasions and vary your choice of hostelry.[1]

WALK TWO
Haunted Taverns

1. Hole in the Wall
2. The Royal Oak
3. The Golden Slipper
4. Black Swan
5. Golden Fleece
6. Cock and Bottle
7. The Whippet Inn
8. Lendal Cellars
9. Punchbowl
10. Ye Olde Starre Inne
11. Roman Bath
12. Old White Swan
13. Snickleway Inn
14. Guy Fawkes Inn
15. Dean Court Hotel
16. The York Arms

Asides

1. The Four Alls Inn
2. The Ebor Inn

Don't stray from the path

3. The Watergate Inn
4. The Windmill Inn

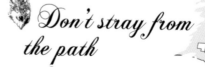

A GUIDED WALK
AROUND THE STREETS
AND TAVERNS OF

HAUNTED YORK

*O*nce again beginning in the vicinity of Bootham Bar, a very short stroll up High Petergate with the bar behind you will allow our inaugural destination to present itself to you on the left.

HOLE IN THE WALL

*M*ake a mental note of the real hole in the wall just before you enter the pub, you'll need to know its location for later on.

The name's origin is in the belief that medieval prisoners, unfortunate enough to have been incarcerated in the nearby Minster jail, were obliged to survive by begging for food from passers by through a hole in the prison wall.

Work being done in 1816 uncovered another hole that led to what appeared to be a personal dungeon, replete with manacles and chains.

As is the case with many an old building in York there was a legend detailing a secret tunnel that ran from the tavern cellar to the York Minster (a similar tale is told about the Golden Slipper) and a tunnel was indeed uncovered but the sounds of ghostly footsteps emanating from its gloomy depths resulted in a panic stricken labourer bricking it up. The eerie sound of footfall can, at times, still be heard.

There have also been reports of a white mist manifesting behind the bar and also the ghostly appearances of both men and woman. It has been speculated that they may be apparitions of the former prisoners, although this is problematic as no details seem to have been given as to their actual appearance.

eaving our ghostly prisoners behind, if you turn right out of the front door and immediately right again you'll be entering the first of a number of York's famous snickets that crop up during the walk. This one is known as Little Peculiar Lane, the name having been bestowed upon it by way of its entrance to the Minster precinct and the word peculiar meaning property, rather than weird (unlike most of York).

Turn right when you exit Dean Park and after a short walk take the first left into the fabulously old and cobbled street that is Ougleforth. Follow the road around the 90 degree turn to the right and before rounding the corner you will see the entrance to Grays Court to your left, a grade 1 listed building with parts that date back to 1080 (see page 17). Head to the end of Ougleforth, noting as you go the

seventeenth-century Dutch House on your right, and turn right into Goodramgate, one of many streets whose name betrays the legacy of York's Viking occupation; 'Gate', derived from the Norse word 'gata' means street. A few doors along on the right you will see our second destination;

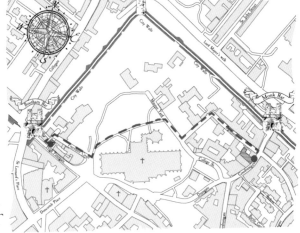

2. Hole in the Wall to
The Royal Oak

THE ROYAL OAK

A grade 2 listed building the Royal Oak was at one time, as with many of York's oldest pubs, a coaching inn named The Blue Boar (not to be confused with the current Blue Boar pub in Castlegate) and boasts a splendid Tudor frontage; although despite the pub's age this didn't materialise until the nineteenth century.

A number of spectres have apparently made the Oak their home, including a tall, gaunt looking gentleman who favours the bar at the rear of the establishment and a woman who has been described, perhaps unkindly, as 'an old prostitute' who appears, perhaps as a result of some ancient altercation with the aforementioned gentleman, to be happier in the front bar.

Children playing by the fire have been reported and the ghost of a young girl has been witnessed in the bar area by some of the regulars.

Not content with these otherworldly residents there are two women who haunt the upstairs of the pub; one who is named Alice, who resides on the first floor, and the other named Mary, who has made herself comfortable in the tavern's upstairs apartment.

In 2009 a former landlady informed the Northern Ghost Investigations team that she had witnessed two dark figures moving past the internal glazed door on route for the bar, only to subsequently discover that the bar was empty.

Turning right out of the pub's entrance you will immediately encounter our next destination.

THE GOLDEN SLIPPER

Next door to the Royal Oak and complete with its own resident ghost by the name of George, the Golden Slipper is a fine old grade 2 listed building built in either the fifteenth or sixteenth century. During some renovation work undertaken in 1984, a mediaeval leather slipper was discovered within one of the walls, an apparently (given the number reported[1]) common ritual that was thought to either bestow fertility on the residence or, possibly more likely, act as a deterrent to demons, witches and ghosts (obviously nobody told George). The slipper is on display in a cabinet in the front room where there is also evidence in the form of a lower ceiling of a 'coffin drop'. Another old custom that held the belief in it being bad luck for a body to be removed from a building through the front door, and so the drop was created to allow the coffin to be lowered into the side passage.

THE FOUR ALLS INN

Compelling sighting given York's strong connection with Dick Turpin (see page 31) as the ghost was a highwayman.

The witness was returning home from their place of work by car when they saw a man dressed in the manner of the notorious thief sitting astride a horse beside the pub. After passing the building and its loitering horseman the driver looked in the rear view mirror and both horse and rider had disappeared.

Turning right out of the Slipper, continue up Goodramgate and you will see on the other side of the road an entrance to a passageway that will take you into the area known as Bedern, an Anglo Saxon word meaning 'house of prayer'. Replete with its own harrowing tale of ghostly children if you follow Bartle Garth to the right the path will take you past the renovated Bedern Hall, originally part of the College of the Vicars Choral and built as a fourteenth-century canteen for the vicars. Reaching the street's end you will see directly opposite you a small snicket. Head into it and when you emerge you can continue straight ahead down Spen Lane which will lead you to Peasholme Green. As you near the end of Spen Lane our next tavern of haunted interest will appear on the opposite side of the road, a beacon of ancient York amidst a sprawl of modern development that has taken place around it.

3. The Golden Slipper to the Black Swan

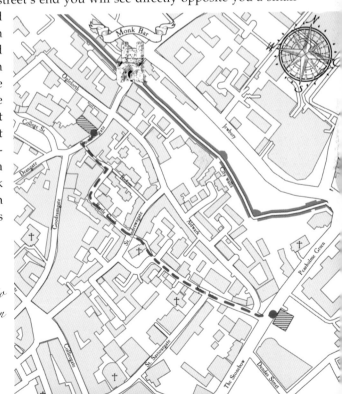

THE BLACK SWAN

Although built in 1417 it was the mid eighteenth century before it became a pub, during which time there were also structural alterations. However, it appears not to have changed at all since then and walking through the solid oak door at the pub's front entrance is akin to stepping back in time.

As with the Hole in the Wall, an old legend stated that a secret tunnel ran from the house, although this one only went as far as St Cuthbert's church on the other side of the road. Up until relatively recently the only clue to the possible existence of this passageway was the decidedly odd presence of a number of descending steps in one of the building's cupboards. They extended a short distance before coming to an abrupt halt at a brick wall. However, during renovations being undertaken in 2003, workmen were required to pull up part of the floor, at which point they discovered an old brick floor that disappeared into the darkness.

A regular spectral visitor is a gentleman in a bowler hat who walks around the pub as though expecting to meet somebody but invariably just disappears. There is also a young woman, her face hidden with long, black hair and attired in a suitably gothic white dress who reportedly does little more than stare vacantly into the fire. Finally, there have been reports from no other person than the landlord himself, who has witnessed a pair of disembodied male legs walking around his accommodation. One can't help but wonder if the pub has a high turnover of innkeepers.

4. Black Swan to the Golden Fleece

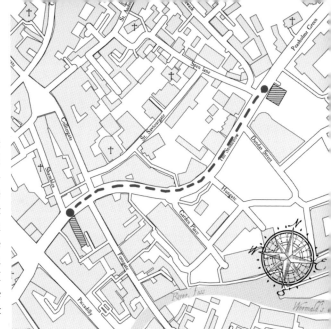

Turning left out of that solid front door will take you back in the direction of the town centre and if you stay on the left hand side of the road you will, before long, see a large golden sheep hanging from the side of a building. Not, I hasten to add, a living ovine but the sign of our next haunted tavern.

GOLDEN FLEECE

York's 'most haunted pub'. A fabulously crooked building owing to its lack of solid foundations the establishment is also a pub of considerable pedigree, with a reference to the building in the York archives as far back as 1503 when it was owned by The Merchant Adventurers. Their primary trade being wool resulted in the pub's appellation, and records show that it was licensed as far back as 1668. It became a popular coaching inn during the early part of the eighteenth century when it was under the ownership of John Peckitt, the Lord Mayor of York. The Mayor's wife, Lady Alice Peckett, gave her name to the yard at the rear of the pub and the street that accesses the yard is now also known by her name. Her ghost has been seen on a number of occasions, usually in the early hours of the morning, and shares the labyrinthine corridors with a woman attired in a Victorian dress, who vanishes through the wall into the shop next door. A Canadian airman by the name of Geoff Monroe came to a violent end when he fell from an upstairs room and whose latent spirit has been witnessed by a number of people. Claims have also been made by persons who have felt a small boy pulling at their legs when they've been sitting down. It may not be the only leg pulling going on but at least one individual claimed to have seen the ghost of 'One Eyed Jack', suitably attired in sixteenth or seventeenth century costume and there has also been a report of a woman dressed in black in the St Catherine's Room.

Arguably deserving of more credence is the claim by Susanne Taggart that she photographed the ghost of a former landlord who hanged himself in the rear bar. Unaware of the spectral presence at the time of taking the photograph, her partner noticed a dark area with a distinctly humanoid shape that doesn't require a great deal of imagination to view as a man pulling a pint. There is apparently a hook hidden behind the false ceiling above the bar that is allegedly the scene of the suicide, although history has not, as yet, related the identity of the man or when the grisly incident took place. One can only hope the spectacle wasn't witnessed by a full bar of expectant but consequently disappointed drinkers.

THE WATERGATE INN

Known as Green Jenny, she has apparently been seen only once and that was as far back as the early eighteenth century. At that time there was an additional room above the front of the property, the entrance to which was gated and the floor of which was earth. The manner of this room strongly suggests its use for the bloodsports of rat baiting and cock fighting, both made illegal by the Cruelty to Animals Act passed in 1835.

Just prior to these activities being banned, an Ostler (a stableman) in the employ of the pub was passing the front of the building when he saw a woman on the staircase that gave access to this room. She was wearing a vivid green dress and he was taken aback at the sight of a lady apparently about to enter an exclusively male area.

In the moment that he acknowledged her and received a wave in return he was of the mind that she was the innkeeper's wife. However, on consideration, he realised that she was a serving girl from the inn, a girl named Jenny who had died.

5. Golden Fleece to the Cock and Bottle

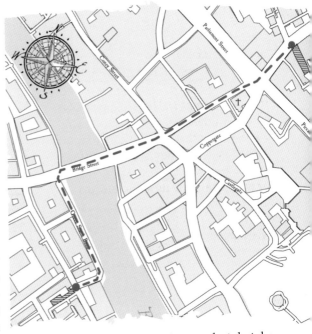

Turning left when leaving the Golden Fleece, you are now faced with a stroll over Skeldergate Bridge and a walk up the side of the River Ouse, a timely opportunity to take some air and also visit the aforementioned Lady Peckett's Yard, the access to which you will see very quickly on your left. Signposted above a veritable hole in the wall, stay alert as it is easy to miss the entrance to one of the spookiest streets you'll have the pleasure to encounter within York. It's not very long so will be but a brief interlude to your journey but do take a walk down to the bottom and as you turn around to return to the safety and light of the bustling street you have left behind, you will see the snicket from it's optimum position. It always sends a bit of a cold shiver down the spine, even if the Lady herself is nowhere to be seen.

Once safely returned to the top, turn left into Stonebow and continue along the path you abandoned until you reach the crossroads of Parliament Street and Piccadilly. Straight ahead of you the road forks with Coppergate, home of the magnificent Jorvik Viking centre, to the left and High Ousegate to the right. Follow the right hand path to the top and cross the busy road into Low Ousegate (there is a pedestrian crossing to assist you in this slightly daunting prospect) and, taking the left hand side of the street, continue forward and Skeldergate Bridge will be upon you within seconds. A glance to the left will take your view up King's Staith where it may rest upon the famous King's Arms Pub, although not, alas, famous for ghosts but for its propensity to flood whenever the Ouse raises by the slightest amount. That said, it is the gathering point for the highly recommended Original Ghost Walk of York.

Having crossed Ouse Bridge you will see a set of steps to your left that will take you down onto Queen's Staith. Descend the steps and continue straight ahead along the river and at the end, turn right and our next destination will be ahead of you.

COCK AND BOTTLE

*W*hose resident spook is thought to be that of the seventeenth century nobleman George Villiers, the second Duke of Buckingham. Villiers was a close childhood friend of King Charles II but seemed to spend most of his life engaging in behaviour designed to annoy and embarrass him, including indulging in an affair with the Countess of Shrewsbury and subsequently shooting her husband in a duel. Amongst his many skills and interests was the art and science of alchemy. He told the theologian Thomas Burnet that he was very close to finding the philosophers stone, a substance that could transmute base metal into gold and provide the elixir of life. It is thought that although he lived in Helmsley he had a laboratory on or near the site of the Cock and Bottle and may have spent a good portion of the time following his retirement from Parliament in the quest for regaining his youth. Although his apparition is not particularly well formed he has been seen on a number of occasions, dressed in suitably refined clothing, but only by women. A former landlady saw him when she was taking a shower and a number of additional young woman have reported being stroked or fondled. He has also been seen sitting by the fire.

There have also been sightings of 'an ugly man' which would suggest an additional phantom as Villiers was known to be an attractive man. There have also been reports of ghostly noises including the sound of a breaking door.

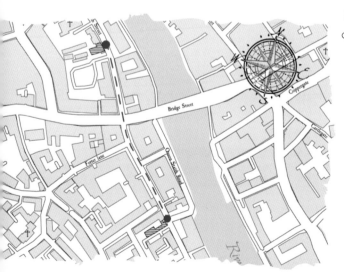

*L*eaving the ghostly Villiers to his alchemical machinations you must turn left onto Skeldergate and follow it to the top. Go straight on over the road into North Street and after a walk of about a hundred yards our next tavern will appear to on the left.

6. Cock and Bottle to the Whippet Inn

THE WHIPPET INN

*A*number of name changes and a complete revision in 2013 may have resulted in our spirit deserting the establishment as there seems to be no recent record of him. Previously named as the Yorkshire Hussar, First Hussar and then the Tap & Spile, a cloaked man was witnessed by a group of men undertaking some decorating during its days as the First Hussar. Witnessed by all present, he apparently strolled through the pub and vanished through a wall.

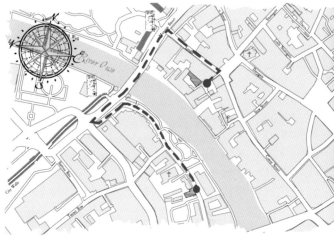

7. The Whippet Inn to Lendal Cellars

WINDMILL INN

Not within the city walls (just) so not on the walk but it has got two fantastic ghosts so we felt it would be highly remiss of us not to give it a mention.

After a major refurbishment in 2010 the Windmill is very much a sports bar these days so not sure if the ghosts are still around but a number of previous landlords have attested to the presence of a man sporting (sorry) a ball and chain (I know, a ball and chain!) which, perhaps unsurprisingly, makes a lot of noise in the cellar.

The second apparition is a small girl who has been seen in the upstairs part of the Inn and is thought to be the ghost of a child that was killed in a coach accident in the late nineteenth century. Staff members have apparently been advised that should they find her a little too vexatious they can open a window and she'll leave.

urning left out of the Whippet and continuing up North Street you will arrive at the base of the bridge. In front of you will be an arch, the other side of which, on the left, is a stairway that will lead you up onto the top of the bridge. Ascend the steps, turn left and then left again and after a walk of about a hundred yards cross over over the road and there will be a turning right into the street known as Lendal. Walk to the end of Lendal and you will emerge into St Helen's Square, home of the famous Bettys Café tea rooms, the Guild Hall and the Lord Mayor's residence, known as the Mansion House (see page 40). If you look to your right, in between the Mansion House and the post office, there is an entranceway to our next tavern with its name proudly displayed on the archway above;

LENDAL CELLARS

grade 2 listed building the pub is housed in the former wine cellar of the Lord Mayor (one hopes he has a new one) and the ceiling is ornately supported by brick vaulting. It shares a boundary wall with the mediaeval Common Hall Lane (see page 104) and is within an area of such historical interest that it has been designated a York Area of Archaeological Importance.

There are remains below the Cellars of a mediaeval Augustinian Friary, housing around 35 monks and boasting a library of over 2000 tomes. Built around 1272 the monastery fell victim to Henry VIII's Dissolution of the Monasteries in 1538 and the ghostly male figures that have been seen in the lower areas of the pub have inevitably been attributed to the expelled monks, perhaps returning to their former homes now that death has enabled them safely to do so. A marked feature of the ghosts is not that they wear habits, but that if you see them and then glance away, upon returning your gaze the person will have vanished.

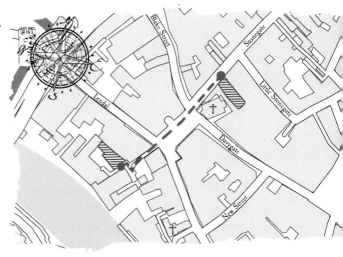

tanding at the top of the incline that took you down to Lendal Cellars you will see in front of you St Helen's Square. On the far side to the left is the bottom of Stonegate, central to the city centre's layout and six feet above the old Roman road that connected the fortress to the River Ouse and its bridge to the settlement on the far side. Shortly after entering Stonegate you will see on your right our next port of call and also the meeting point for Trevor Rooney's Ghost walk.

THE PUNCHBOWL

ow beamed ceilings and dark wood panelling certainly create a suitably atmospheric environment and there are at least three ghosts said to inhabit the old rooms and cellar. A former landlord who died in a fire has been heard descending the cellar steps and a strange, disembodied glowing head has been seen floating just above the floor of the back room.

Below this back room is the cellar, which at some point was lowered from six foot to five, suggesting that it is either the head of the landlord, continuing on after reaching the foot of the stairs, with the remainder of his ghostly body hidden beneath the floor, or it is the apparition of a six foot tall man who apparently died in the cellar shortly before the ceiling was lowered.

Somewhat more frantic ghostly footsteps have also been heard on the floorboards above people's heads. These are thought to belong to a girl who worked at the pub at a time when it was also acting as a brothel. Having made the fatal error of resisting the attention of a drunken client, he pursued her from room to room, eventually throttling her to death. The sound of her last, desperate minutes, as she attempts to evade her nemesis, seem to have been recorded into the fabric of the building. Thumping noises emanating from the walls of the top bedroom, accompanied by a perpetual chill even on warm days, have been attributed by staff

to the hostile spirit of the man responsible for her death. Even more alarming were the experiences of a previous landlady, who claimed to have been roughly pulled across the room as a result of the ghost seizing her hair, and a chef, who hastily exited the building after a ghost tried to strangle him.

Somewhat less malicious is poltergeist activity in the form of glasses being pushed off various surfaces, doors being opened and closed and tables and chairs mysteriously re-arranging themselves when the pub is empty. These have all been attributed to the spectral presence of a fisherman who frequented the establishment regularly during the nineteenth century. Although no one knows his actual name he is usually referred to as Frederick.

There is also the ubiquitous 'grey lady', in this case the forlorn spirit of a rejected woman who took her own life. Even death has not brought her peace as she repeatedly returns in the hope of finding her lost lover.

    *C*ontinuing your walk up Stonegate our next destination's entrance is very easy to miss. As such, you are advised to look up where you will easily see a large advertising banner stretching over the street. Below it to the left is the entrance to the banner's subject:

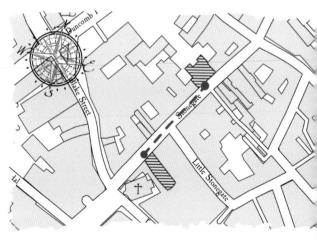

9. Punchbowl to Ye Olde Starre Inn

YE OLDE STARRE INNE

    *Y*ork's oldest licensed pub, Ye Olde Starre Inne[1] was built in the sixteenth century, although the cellars may date back as far as the tenth.

The Civil War brought the pain of the locally-fought Battle of Marston Moor in 1644 to the inn when the Roundheads used it as a billet hospital and morgue despite the royalist sympathies and annoyance of the landlord, William Foster. The desperate cries of the wounded and dying have been heard all round the pub and the screams of the makeshift operating theatre still emanate from the ancient cellar.

A royalist officer provides an imposing consummation to this rather grisly backdrop although none have reported him to be injured.

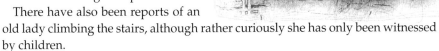

There is also a story concerning two cats that were apparently bricked up alive in the pillar that separates the bar from the door. People have heard them running through the bar and dogs bark and make futile attempts to reach them through the pillar.

There have also been reports of an old lady climbing the stairs, although rather curiously she has only been witnessed by children.

Coming back out of the snicket that led you into the Starre you will see on the other side of the street (and slightly to the left) another snicket. This is the entrance to Coffee Yard and an area that was once home to a thriving print industry, evidenced by the small red devil that watches over the portal (see page 98).

Head down the snicket and you quickly emerge into the yard where the rather excellent Barley Hall stands. A reconstructed medieval townhouse saved from demolition in the '80s, there are parts of the building that date back to 1360.

Continue across the yard and on through the snicket and you will find yourself in Grape Lane. Walk straight ahead for a few yards and take the first right and then

10. Ye Old Starre Inne to the Roman Bath

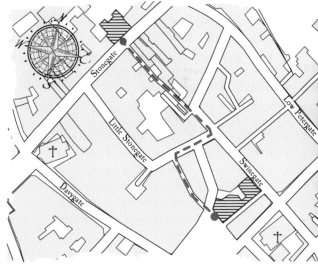

immediately look to your left, where you will see a tiny thoroughfare by the name of Finkle Street that connects Back Swinegate to St Sampson's Square. At the other end of this street turn left and you will be outside our next tavern.

ROMAN BATH

A pub that is as keen on live music as it is on the archaeological heritage that gives it its name. Unsurprisingly considering the seventeen hundred year time span since their occupation, there is very little remaining of the Roman presence. However, for a small fee you can go below the Roman Bath inn and stand amid the remains of a caldarium, or steam bath and also the remains of a neighbouring plunge bath. These were discovered in 1930 during renovation work and there is also a small museum with Roman-related exhibits. Various ghostly experiences have been reported by visitors including the sound of footsteps and also the sound of splashing water. A decorator painting the walls at the foot of the staircase that leads into the baths refused to continue, claiming that "something was there" and a couple in 2006 reported feeling a presence and capturing a strange light anomaly on their mobile phone camera. Perhaps the most extraordinary experience was that of a previous landlord and a friend who, in the early nineties, took it upon themselves to stay the night in the baths as a means of raising money for charity and also raising awareness of the pub and its ancient remains. As the men were settling down for the night ahead they both witnessed the same thing: an extremely bright light that was accompanied by the figure of a person. The manifestation did not last long and appeared to fade out into the area occupied by the excavated 'cold-room', although one of the men witnessed the light again a fortnight later. The cynics amongst you may be wondering whether the whole thing was made up by the landlord as a publicity stunt, in which case it's worth pointing out that following this incident he resigned.

11. Roman Bath to the Old White Swan

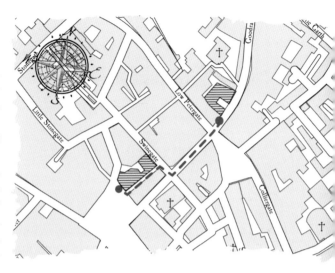

Turn left out of the Roman Bath and the Three Cranes snicket will be seen very quickly on you left. Head up this and turn right at the end and then left. You'll now be in Church Street and heading towards the crossroads of Low Petergate. Go straight on into Goodramgate and on your left will be the courtyard of our next hostelry;

OLD WHITE SWAN

The pub occupies a space once taken up by nine different buildings that originally were home to a diverse range of occupants, including a barber, a poultry market and a pigsty. By the end of the eighteenth century it had become a major coaching inn with stabling for about thirty horses. A relic from this time in the form of four steps known as 'mountings' can still be seen in the entrance courtyard and were used by passengers for boarding and disembarking from the coaches. The parish records of 1723 make note of the instruction to local constables to be vigilant of the illegal activities of the papists, supporters of the Roman Catholic church that were still being persecuted as a result of the Reformation and would gather in secret to discuss their recusant beliefs. The Old White Swan is thought to have been one of their meeting places and staff have reported ghostly occurrences with chairs, that would be found in a circle around the fire which would have mysteriously lit itself. On one occasion chairs were seen flying around in the air before suddenly crashing to the floor and people have reported ghostly voices talking to each other.

12. Old White Swan to the Snickleway Inn

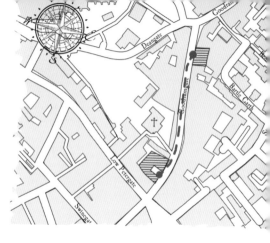

Turn left out of the Old White Swan and continue along Goodramgate. At the other end of the street look to your right and before long you should see a magnificently eerie pub sign depicting the alleyway that gives our next tavern its name.

SNICKLEWAY INN

The name is actually a different spelling of the word 'Snickelway', which is in itself a made up word by author Mark Jones for a splendid book he published in 1983 detailing all the passages and alleyways that snake through the centre of York.[1]

Dating back to the late fifteenth century and renovated in the late sixteenth century the pub boasts a number of ghosts including a four-year-old girl who was the victim of a tragic accident involving a brewer's dray, and a woman by the name of Mrs Tulliver, who is kept company by her spectral cat.

There is also an old man who has been seen walking through the pub and then

dematerialising and an Elizabethan man dressed in a blue doublet who has been seen standing behind the bar.

Another example of poltergeist activity occurs within the cellar when barmen have had spanners thrown at them and there have been a number of reports of a strong smell of lavender that permeates the inn. It has been suggested that the latter is connected to the outbreaks of plague that hit York in 1604 and 1631 when lavender was used to mask the stench of the dead and dying victims.

In addition, there is the ghost of Marmaduke Buckle, who has been seen occasionally in one of the first floor rooms and also seen from the outside of the pub staring down into Goodramgate from the window. Marmaduke actually lived with his wealthy parents next door to the pub at the turn of the eighteenth century and by all accounts was a deeply unhappy young man. Afflicted with a number of physical handicaps he was shunned and persecuted by his peers and eventually felt so wretched that he saw death as his only escape. Carving into the wall plaster his name, the year of his birth and adding what was to be the year of his death, he then hanged himself from a wooden beam.

13. Snickleway Inn to the Guy Fawkes Inn

In an attempt to find a slightly more cheery historical setting let us turn right out of the Snickleway Inn and head to the end of this section of Goodramgate. Turn left into Deansgate, where the formidable view of the Minster's eastern aspect will be to your right and Minster Close will be ahead. Follow Minster Close along the southern part of the cathedral and emerging into Minster Yard you will see directly opposite its south transept entrance, which incorporates the rather marvellous sixteenth-century Rose Window, a turning left into Minster Gates. A short street, you will very quickly turn right at the end of it and proceed up High Petergate.

On the left you will see the entrance to one of the more atmospheric haunted taverns that we have enjoyed visiting.

THE GUY FAWKES INN

The birth place of Guy Fawkes, is now a rather splendid and spooky place to enjoy a drink and although Fawkes himself has yet to make an appearance a woman dressed in Victorian clothing has been seen in one of the bedrooms. She was described as relatively young with long hair and a slim build. Less conventional as far as ghostly manifestations go is the claim in 2009 by Paranormal Investigation group Ghostcircle that they caught the materialisation of the then recently deceased pop star Michael Jackson on camera.

In addition, quite a number of guests have reported strange occurrences such as televisions turning themselves on at night and the Belfry Suite allegedly has two resident phantoms in the form of children who were victims of cholera.

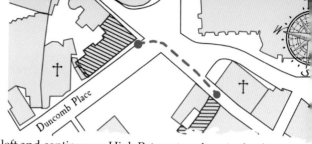

14. Guy Fawkes Inn to the Dean Court Hotel

*L*eaving the gas lit old world charm of the Guy Fawkes Inn, turn left and continue up High Petergate, where in the distance you will be able to see the point where our journey originally began. However, although the end may be in sight there are still two more taverns we have yet to frequent. Crossing over Duncombe Place with the view of the front of the Minster to your right you will see ahead of you, across the road, the first of these two establishments, a suitably dignified bar to help ease what by now may be a rather nervous disposition on your part back into a more conventional frame of mind.

Although it is, of course, haunted.

DEAN COURT HOTEL

*D*ating back to 1855 the hotel was originally three separate buildings built by the Minster to house its clergy. Sightings of a woman in the basement have been attributed to a 'mad maid', although there seems to be no information as to who this unfortunate person is or why she is mad. One can't help but speculate as to a possible connection to 'Mad Alice', whose existence seems to be entirely fictional with the exception of a street named after her (see page 52). Perhaps she did exist and worked at the hotel.

Room 36 has become somewhat notorious over the years with strange feelings being reported, a distinct cold spot and something being witnessed by three guests in the bathroom mirror.

A roman soldier has been seen strolling the hotel corridors in a potential echo of the famous Treasurer's House story (see page 14). The Roman road that was built for transporting materials for the original fortress, located on the site of the current Minster, runs from the Guildhall by the river and underneath the Dean Court Hotel. Remains off a Roman backstreet that connected the Praetorium to the basilica have been unearthed during excavations by the York Archaeological Trust and evidence of a Roman barracks was unearthed as long ago as

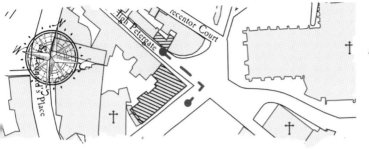

the sixties, so perhaps the only surprising element to the story is that he seems to be the only one.

*A*fter emerging from the Dean Court, turn left and then left again and you will see, on the opposite side of the street.

YORK ARMS

A minor note of warning; take care not to be hit by the vintage cyclist that manifests on the street outside the York Arms. Visible only to children, he is identifiable by his old fashioned (historical specifics unavailable at this point) clothing and rides an equally dated bicycle.

Having safely entered the York Arms, you are faced with the choice of a somewhat compact bar at the front of the pub, or the relative anonymity of a much larger bar to the left. A former Georgian Chapter Coffee House, the spirits that visit this pub seem to have wandered out of their proper haunts and gone for a walk. One is a blurry grey lady who is the sad remnant of a nun punished for the unfortunate act of becoming pregnant by being walled up in a nearby church building. A little confusingly, this may be the same figure that a number of witnesses have testified to as being a young woman, an old woman and a child.

An unknown woman apparently pops up at unexpected moments in the gents' toilets (not that there would ever be expected moments) and became so annoying to one former landlord while he was trying to decorate that he threw a paintbrush at her. It is thought that she may be the same ghost that haunts the Theatre Royal which is close by.

There have also been reports of poltergeist activity resulting in objects being moved or even thrown, doors apparently opening and closing or even locking themselves, and ashtrays being tipped over.

By Way of Introduction…

Granted that the title of the humble but nonetheless aspiring publication you clutch inquiringly in your hands will afford a none too subtle indication as to the main theme of its endeavour, notably to guide and educate the inquisitive reader as to the particulars of York's phantom occurrences, it would be nothing short of a gross negligence on my part to allow a misconstruction that, if unchecked, may lead to the belief that this is our sole topic of concern.

While ghosts, poltergeists and all things of a spiritualist nature are the particular components of the otherworldly realm that continually pique our curiosity (and it would be difficult for such a thing to be avoided when one lives in Europe's most haunted city) our intrigue is by no means limited to those themes, and I have endeavoured, in a manner that I sincerely hope is not too presumptuous, to catalogue a number of noteworthy elements to a selection of topics that may, at the very least, keep you mildly diverted.

Should any aspect of your scholarly endeavour necessitate a desire to contact us there are a number of alternative methods that will facilitate such an endeavour and they can all be found at the rear of this very tome.

George Crowquill
Purkess Esq.

1. Common Hall Lane Ghost
2. Haunting of Laurence Sterne
3. The Red Devil
4. Thomas Gent

1. York Castle Museum

GHOSTS OF YORK

AN INTRODUCTION BY THE EMINENT PUBLISHER, AUTHOR AND SPIRIT SEEKER, GEORGE CROWQUILL PURKESS ESQ.

Although frequently in a state if disquietude as a result of the ever sanguine quest for evidence of the beyond, I feel it cannot be overly optimistic on my part to assume that you, dear reader, have an interest in ghosts. I therefore present to you, in the full hope and expectation that it will act as a complement to the audacious journey you are undertaking, an introduction (for the subject at hand is far too prodigious to attempt a comprehensive revue, hence the walks and accompanying tales detailed in the primary pages of this very book) to the ghosts of York.

However, I must inevitably begin with a question: Where, I ask (fully in the knowledge that your resultant confused stare is little more than I would extend myself should such a question be proposed) should one begin? I suggest, if I may be so bold, a place where at least in our unnerved minds we may be calmed by the heady mix of a fine ale or wine; the tavern. There was a time dear reader, long before the days of recent memory (especially if one has indulged in too much calming of the mind) when the city of York had enough taverns within its walls to service an easily bored imbiber with a fresh venue for each day of the year. Despite those heady days being little more than a sublime memory there is, by way of consolation for the intrepid occultist, undoubtedly a ghost for each day of the year, and few would dare to disagree that this estimate is most assuredly an understatement.

From the gatherings of legionnaires during York's antiquity to the present-day meanderings atop the Bar Wall, there have been a profusion of supernatural occurrences that have become as much a part of York's legacy as the Romans themselves: poltergeists; demon dogs; mischievous children; kings, queens, lords and ladies ; the pestilent, the poor and the crippled; murdered and murderers; and, most famously, the spectral manifestation of those very Roman legionnaires hitherto alluded to. The churches are haunted, even York Minster itself; as are the shops, museums, libraries, courts, theatres, restaurants, the streets, even York Dungeon has its ghosts; and so too, of course, do the taverns.

Lamentably, many of these places are no longer practical to investigate. certainly not in person. Those that are museums have delicate artefacts and retail outlets with valuable (at least to some) stock while others are dwelling places containing residents who express an understandable reluctance to the suggestion of a group of marauding spook-seekers traipsing through their property. The King's Manor is now part of the University of York, yet amongst its beautiful stonework there are phantoms in abundance: seventeenth-century casualties of the first English Civil War jostle for spectral space with the likes of Henry Hastings; the Earl of Huntingdon; the Black Abbot; Thomas Wentworth, Earl of Strafford and even one of Henry VIII's tragic queens, Catherine Howard.

However, let us not be too downhearted at this rather depressing state of affairs. As has oft been demonstrated and attested it is sufficient merely to attend a number of these locations within the daylight hours so as to at the vey least gain a perception of the nature of its preternatural ambience. Periodically, if one is blessed with exceptional fortune, a manifestation will occur during this period, begging the question: are the ghosts actually aware of the hour of the day? As an example, the splendidly monikered Sarah Brocklebank haunts the medieval Micklegate Bar, and has no compulsion with regard to making her presence known either by day or night.[1] In addition there is the haunting at The Antiques Centre on Stonegate, reputably the responsibility of a further young lady by the name of Laura Hodgson, daughter of York's Gas Engineer during the reign of Queen Victoria; she has appeared to staff during the daylight hours on a number of occasions. On a more scandalous note, the lecherous George Villiers, 2nd Duke of Buckingham, made his presence felt to the female staff and visitors of the Cock & Bottle tavern on Skeldergate for a good number of years whenever the urge overcame him. Recent years have born witness to a decline in reports but we are ever vigilant as to the reappearance of this groping ghost!

The Eboracum Legion Bathhouse, now a subterranean element of the Roman Bath tavern,[2] is home to a supernatural presence that equally has no issue with prowling the site at whichever period of the day suits its desire. Visitors to what is now a museum have reported sights, sounds and an experience of being in the company of something otherworldly; much the same experience has also been recorded at the Richard III Museum in Monk Bar.[3]

If the opportunity for first hand investigation presents itself it will no doubt become apparent to the more discerning amongst you that some of these reports are, if one were to be generous, exaggerated. However, many of the reports are not so easy to dismiss and if you'll forgive the return to the subject of York's taverns we find the perpetuation of a palpable contest to claim right to the accolade: 'York's Most Haunted Pub' (I myself have spent many a diverting hour attempting to assist with this particular disputation). Notable participants include the Golden Fleece, also laying claim to being the longest-sited tavern in York[4] and hosting a number of spectres including the Lord Mayor's wife, Alice Peckett, reputedly a visitor from her residence next door.[5] In addition, there are reports of a number of visitations witnessed walking through walls and also, most curiously, floating heads. There is also Ye Olde Starre Inne on Stonegate, the third longest continuously licensed pub in York, bedevilled by wounded soldiers, black cats and a little old lady and not a stone's throw from the equally haunted Punch Bowl, that may also lay claim to a profusion of ghosts.

Lady Peckitt's Yard
Photograph by Vincent Danks

A further contender is the Snickleway Inn on Goodramgate, with the additional attraction of a most remarkable tavern sign, that is home to a plethora of ghosts manifesting as sights, sounds, smells and feelings of innate evil. The apparitions at the York Arms on High Petergate have been documented for many years and, more recently, the York Brewery building on Toft Green has itself become a centre for paranormal activity, demonstrating that York's supernatural heritage is not merely a bygone idiosyncrasy but a continuing and evolving phenomenon.

I implore you to indulge and enjoy that which York has to offer and should you be fortunate enough to experience any form of supernatural occurrence during your travels around this ancient city, please do not hesitate to share the details of said encounter with the publisher, that we may consider it suitable for publication in a future edition.

1. Situated to the south of the city, Micklegate Bar is the royal gateway to the city and contains a museum: the Henry VII Experience.
2. If the sound of a live musical troop excites you then pray be aware of the Roman Bath's most notable programme of events available for perusal via: www.tizyorkmusic.com.
3. This bar is located to the north of the city.
4. The Golden Fleece, whose name derives from one of the city's prominent trades of the thirteenth to the seventeenth century, is mentioned in the City Archives of 1503.
5. Although known as Lady Peckett, Alice Peckett was not a member of the aristocracy, for in York there was a tradition regarding Lord Mayors and their spouses: "He is lord for a year and a day. She is lady for ever and aye").

IS THE CASTLE MUSEUM HAUNTED?
GHOSTLY APPARITIONS AND UNEARTHLY NOISES
A historical overview and reporting of witness statements and photographic evidence

Having been labelled with the somewhat dramatic epitaph of 'the most haunted city in Europe' it should therefore come as little surprise that contained within its medieval walls are numerous public buildings, dwellings and streets that an unnerving number of ghosts have determined to take up eternal residence, often vying for a single location.

As such, when putting quill to paper in an endeavour to document such spectral occurrences, one is forced into the unenviable position of being unsure as to where to commence.

However, never let it be said that an uncertainty of mind has ever resulted in an admission of defeat. Let us visit (at least for the moment in a metaphorical sense) the locality of the York Castle Museum. Situated on the south side of the River Foss and adjacent to the main highway known as Tower Street he museum faces Clifford's Tower, a surviving keep following the thirteenth century re-development of the site by Henry III.

Given the name of the museum a continued lack of bewilderment will result from the knowledge that the site was originally home to a heavily fortified castle that can lay claim to a history as involved and troubled as that of York's own.

Originally constructed in 1068 by William the Conqueror in the aftermath of the Norman conquest of York, the castle went though many re-builds and developments until by the end of the fourteenth century the buildings had increasingly become used for the incarceration of both local villains and scoundrels and also for the detainment of political malefactors. By the sixteenth century the tradition of carrying out capital punishment by executing the criminal at Micklegate Bar had switched to hanging the wretched victim from the top of Clifford's Tower.

In the preceeding years of the Restoration an expansion to the county facilities in the bailey was undertaken and improvements to the Grand Jury House and the Common Hall were also carried out. However, by the dawn of the eighteenth century the county jail was in a desperate state. As a result, funding was made available from local taxes to re-develop the area using

A sketch of York Castle and its surrounds as it would have appeared in 1730.
1820 watercolour by Mr Waud from Thomas Cooper's *History of York Castle*, published in 1911.

stone that had been extracted from the ruins of St. Mary's Abbey.[1]

Three new buildings were erected and the Assize Courts were constructed. In time, the Female Prison and the County Jail were combined to form the much admired (at the time) Debtor's Prison. However, the felons' wing was clearly not to the same standard and was criticised for not only being of diminutive proportions but for also lacking water. Conditions became so unbearable that a particularly gruesome night in 1739 resulted in the death by suffocation of nine prisoners. As if this were not harrowing enough, the ineffectual castle mills were modernised in 1778 with a steam engine, creating a vast amount of smoke and noise that added considerably to the already miserable conditions of those incarcerated.

The inaugural years of the nineteenth century saw no improvement to the conditions and the situation began to escalate when a growing number of the members of York's more macabre population began turning up to see prisoners being taken for execution. A decision was taken to improve the method by which the convicted were dispatched and the process was moved to the circular area in front of the main buildings known as the Eye of the Ridings (now known as the Eye of York). This had formally been the castle's courtyard, and the 'short drop' method of hanging was introduced which allowed for a much more rapid implementation of the hanging method.

However, this did not silence the critics and further opprobrium was levied at the level of overcrowding that had resulted in occasions when prisoners awaiting execution were being kept in the jail yard for lack of alternative space. The situation culminated in 1821 when an official complaint was made at the assizes and an investigation was begun. In 1825 this led to a new, modern prison being built in a Tudor Gothic style and the executions being moved to the backyard of the Female Prison, were they were concealed from prying eyes by a newly constructed stone wall.

It remained the county prison until 1900 at which point the inmates were of a military rather than domestic nature, staying open until 1929 when its function as a prison was permanently discontinued. The prison buildings were demolished in

1935 and the former Assize Courts building is now, rather appropriately, the home of the York Crown Court.

Which brings us to the original Debtor's Prison and Female Prison that are the subject of this very article, for it is these buildings that are now home to the York Castle Museum and although the history of the site that has been dutifully outlined for your edification is, to say the least, somewhat compacted, I sincerely hope that it has been sufficient to bestow an appreciation as to how the spectral realm should be so infused within it's walls.

Perhaps the most notorious of the criminals that spent their last night within the cramped cells of the Felons' Prison was highway robber and horse thief Dick Turpin. His exploits have been romanticised in the years since his execution on the seventh day of April 1739 to the extent that few people today will be ignorant of his name. Sadly, depending on your point of view, most of the paranormal experiences that have been reported over the years appear to have little or no connection to the notorious murderer.[2]

According to staff who have worked at the museum this honour must go to the sound of people singing. Initially experienced by a local television crew filming in the mock Victorian street of Kirkgate, itself built upon the once Female Prison yard, the noise of women singing was assumed by the film crew to be part of the sound effects tape that constitutes an element of the Victorian era experience.

A museum guide dutifully offered to switch of the offending recording and, as he ascended the stairs, the singing could be quite clearly heard. However, upon reaching the room housing the effects equipment and opening the door the singing abruptly stopped. Furthermore, upon checking the status of the equipment he found it to have already been deactivated.

Subsequently, in a commendable but ultimately futile attempt at fund raising for a worthy charity the Health and Safety Manager offered to spend a full night in the Condemned Cell. Given that this was the very cell that Dick Turpin, amongst a large number of other sentenced villains that been acquainted with the small room, had spent his last night one would have hoped (once again, depending on your point of view) that if anything untoward were to take place that it would be relevant to one of these scoundrels. Alas, this was not to be and our intrepid hero became a further testifier to the sound of voices singing. At first assuming that a roguish colleague was playing a trick upon him he decided that the best course of action would be to locate the source of the noise. Upon conclusion of examining all the conceivable places that were within hearing our hapless philanthropist decided on the notably unheroic act of fleeing to the safety of the museum offices upstairs.

Should you have formed the opinion that an acoustic source has been the sole cause of such worrisome discombobulation, allow me to correct what is unquestionably a misconception. Albeit that nowadays it is commonplace for the museum to be awash with staff in Victorian costume, in the days before the introduction of this entertainment a woman garbed in nineteenth century attire was seen by one of the guides, and no amount of subsequent searching for the lady revealed her to exist. In addition, a small boy in what appears to be a 1930s' or possibly 1940s' outfit has been seen a number of times on the Military Gallery, apparently displaying the unquestionably annoying habit of vanishing around a corner as soon as he is witnessed. A small dog has also been seen on a number of occasions by both staff and visitors alike. One can't help wondering if the frustrated lad is desperately trying to find his pet.

There has also been an occasion when a teacher entrusted to the safe keeping of a school party was sufficiently perturbed by the sight of an elderly woman seated in one of the hearths that she reported the experience to a guide. Upon returning to the hearth the woman had completely vanished.

A potentially exhilarating report was given much attention in the national online press two years ago when some photographs of a family visiting the museum in 2012 seemed to be accompanied by a small girl wearing a Victorian dress. Although subsequently much maligned as being nothing more than the creative use of a mobile phone app I await further news following a possible examination of the prints. However, I fear that Houdini may be turning in his grave.

---

1. Their enthusiasm being fortuitously curbed, one can still admire the remnants of the abbey in the Museum Gardens, entrance from Museum Street.
2. For those of an inquisitive nature, Dick Turpin's alleged grave resides in the grounds of St George's churchyard on Lead Mill Lane.

WADE & THE WITCH AND A HAND FROM OL' NICK

If one is of an adventurous inclination there is a highway that leads from York onto the moors that will eventually take a particularly intrepid traveller to the east coast and the gothic delights of Whitby. However, assuming that the indomitable soul that has embarked upon this most audacious of journeys has done so from a desire to fully appreciate the beauty and mystery of all that the surrounding country has to offer, that person would be nothing short of a fool if a temporary suspension at the natural formation that is know as the Hole of Horcum was not duly observed.

A most singular moorland hollow in the shape of a bowl it is referred to locally as the Devil's Punchbowl and its creation is so firmly rooted in archaic mythology that any attempt to define it's genesis unequivocally would be futile. That said, let us be stout of heart and at the very least make an attempt, for it is a journey into antiquity every bit as intriguing as the beckoning pilgrimage of the Punchbowl itself.

We will begin with the tale that actually seems the least distinguished despite it being responsible for the bowl's informal appellation. It concerns a pact made between the devil and a witch that, rather recklessly on the part of the old crone in question, concluded with the abdication of her soul. Upon meeting the devil on the moor as arranged, the hasty nature and damning consequence of her actions brought about a not altogether surprising change of heart, and the witch decided that a far superior alternative to this arrangement would be to bugger off. Thus, with an alacrity betraying her supernatural power she flew off across the moor along The Old Wife's Way, leaving a rather vexed Satan feeling more than a little cheated. In response, the Devil furiously scooped up handfuls of earth to throw at the fleeing witch but alas, his aim was inadequate and the witch, no doubt cackling, made her escape. It is alleged that the Devil's finger marks are still visible where he tore the earth from the moor and left the bowl and that his inaccurately aimed projectiles formed what is now known as Blakey Topping.[1]

Moving on to what appears to be the most celebrated explanation for this most esteemed of holes is the tale of Wade the giant and his wife Bel. Our large in stature gentleman and his consort lived in the castle at Mulgrave, found himself in what may have been, although documented evidence is lacking in this particular detail, an entirely justified disagreement with his spouse. Upon the realisation that his position in whatever dispute was ensuing was failing to be acknowledged, it apparently became clear that his only recourse was to hurl a gigantic lump of earth at the hapless woman. His duly scooped up fistful of soil created the void that is now the Hole of Horcum. Bel, perhaps as a result of being on the receiving end of earthen projectiles on previous occasions, undertook the most sensible of precautions and ducked, the large lump of earth landing nearby and forming what is now Blakey Ridge.[2]

This rather eccentric couple are also said to be responsible for the construction of Wade's Causeway, also known as 'Old Wife's Trod', 'Auld Wife's Trod', 'Skivik', 'Gateskichewic' and 'Wade's Wife's Causey', an ancient trackway of some 6000 years in age whose actual builders are unknown.[3]

The legend states that Wade, clearly in a more amenable frame of mind, built the causeway so as to allow easy ingress for his wife's regular excursion to the market or pasture with her cow. Interestingly, the exact identity of Wade's companion appears to be little understood. Despite the fact that contemporary accounts of the legend referring to an equally large woman (she carried the stones to build the causeway in her apron) known as Wade's wife would lead to a not unreasonable assumption that they were an association resulting from wedlock, there is some debate within folklorist circles as to whether this was indeed the case.[4]

Antiquarian Hilda Ellis Davidson is of the impression that Bel is in fact the cow, and that no woman exists as part of the legend.[5]

To add to the confusion, the etymology of the word 'wife' can be traced to the middle English word 'Wif', which I am reliably informed simply means 'woman' and therefore, keeping the older names for the track firmly placed within our intellectual frame of reference, 'Old Wife' is actually nothing more than 'Old Woman'. This opens up speculation as to who exactly this woman is (assuming, if you'll pardon the potential defamation, she's not a cow). It has been suggested that Bel is a corruption of the Norse mythological character of Beyla, whose function was that of a milkmaid[6] and given that Wade has a vast amount of myth-ological back story rooted in Norse mythology this is perhaps an understandable approach.[7]

Alternatively, it has also been suggested that Bel is of an equally high stature, not just in physical proportions but also in theological context. An analogy has been made that promotes the concept of Bel as the Gaelic goddess figure Cailleach, who is a multiple aspect deity comprising such diverse elements as hag, mother, warrior and fertility.[8] Given the somewhat exceptional non de plume of this character it is noteworthy that she is not unknown in the Yorkshire regions and that at Rudston, where resides Britain's tallest standing stone, the local mythology advocates the notion of Cailleach being representative of winter, and that with her death on the first day of February each year she makes way for Bride, the youthful aspect of the Irish deity that represents spring.[9]

---

1. It is worth noting that a remarkably analogous tale is attributed to an eminently similar landscape feature in Hindhead in the southern county of Surrey. Furthermore, it is also known as the Devil's Punchbowl.
2. An additional and equally noteworthy destination for the fearless traveller is the Red Lion Inn, Blakey Ridge, a sixteenthth century tavern located at the highest point of the North York Moors National Park.
3. In addition to the various facets of the York Moor, including Freebrough Hill, he is credited (with due assistance from Bel) with the construction of both Mulgrave Castle and Pickering Castle. There is also a well nearby known as Old Wife's Well situated 200 metres from the large prehistoric site known as Mauley Cross.
4. The earliest published source is from 1779.
5. This apparently reflects an earlier British tradition of the bountiful cow, who would generously proffer milk to all who came forward.
6. A further confusion is the suggestion by some authorities that this derives etymologically from baula, meaning cow, creating a somewhat circular argument.
7. https://teessidepsychogeography.wordpress.com
8. Aside from his apparent industrious building capacity and his giant stature, Wade is the English translation of a prominent Norse deity (also known as Vadi (Norse) and Wate (Middle High German)). The oldest known reference is in the Old English poem 'Widsith'. The Þiðrekssaga states that his father was Vilkinus and his mother was a mermaid. Other sources refer to his mother as being a sub-aquatic dwelling giant by the name of Walchilt.
9. Bride is also known as Brigit, Brigid or Brighid, meaning exalted one. She is the daughter of the Dagda and is one of the Tuatha Dé Danann, an ancient supernatural race that populated Ireland.

THE RED DEVIL

In each issue of *Haunted York* we shall endeavour to enlighten our most curious of readers by giving prominence to a notable and mysterious (or at the very least, interesting) feature within the York walls.

It seems appropriate given our documenting elsewhere the trials and ghostly tribulations of York's own Laurence Sterne and his connection with the Stonegate-located print firm of Ann Ward that our initiatory entry should concern a printer's devil.

It is said that a red devil was the traditional sign

The Red Devil, Stonegate, York.
Photograph by Tony Grist

for a print shop[1] and the very house of which the aforementioned Sterne took up residence features a most prominent and colourful example on the outside of its front face. Painted a bright red and sporting a black beard (although perusing old photographs leads one to imagine that this was not always the case) our guardian friend overlooks the entrance to Coffee Yard and marks an area that once housed not just printers but also associated trades such as guild craftsmen. goldsmiths and glass painters.

Although the representation is literal, the actual printer's devils were the young apprentices that would run errands within the print workshop, Such duties would include the preparation of printing ink and the general scurrying around with the metal typefaces used in the presses. A number of notions as to the origin of the term exist, the most likely being that upon the completion of a day's labouring the poor young chaps (for they were almost always male) were covered in so much black ink that their superiors were reminded of the devil, a being often associated in those times with the colour black.

Eight woodcuts illustrating the printing process.
Sixteenth century German

A somewhat droll superstition has also been attributed to the appellation that affirms the existence of a precursor to the gremlin, a creature of supernatural origin that would deliberately alter the type within the presses to create misspelled words or even nonsensical sentences (it is my belief that entire editorial team here at *Haunted York* are familiar with the creature).

An additional tale involves the rather dubious practice of Johann Fust, the business partner of Johann Gutenberg, the German printer responsible for the development of the printing press and subsequent European print revolution. Fust sold a number of copies of the bible to King Louis XI of France that he deviously claimed to be hand written, despite them being printed on a Gutenberg press. When the court officials noticed that all the individual letters were identical, something deemed to be beyond the capabilities of even the most experienced of calligraphers, they accused Fust of conspiring with the Devil. It did not help the matter that elements of the text had been printed using red ink, allowing a further accusation of the use of blood in the tome's creation. Although imprisoned for this blatant act of sacrilegious behaviour Fust was later set free when the actual production process of the bibles was revealed.

It is also worth noting that upon the end of a print run the typefaces used would be discarded into a receptacle known as a 'hellbox'. It was the unenviable task of the devil's printer to sort the letters and replace them in the housing repository known as the job case. It is unclear whether the fanciful appellation 'hellbox' stems from the nickname of the apprentices or vice versa (or indeed, whether it was just a bloody awful job).

---

1.   An interesting peculiarity arose during the necessary research that is the inevitable lot of the scribe in that the 'traditional sign of the printer' only seems to refer to the red devil in York. As yet I have been unable to find any other devil, either extant or recorded in history, that marks the premises of a printer. It is entirely likely that this is naught but a shortcoming on the part of my investigation, and I therefore beg not just forgiveness for this nonfulfillment of obligation, but also humbly ask that should any forgiving reader possess any knowledge of such a devil, that they hastily impart their enviable wisdom by way of the editorial address.

THE HAUNTING OF LAURENCE STERNE

Laurence Sterne was the renowned author of the humorous semi-biographical narrative 'The Life and Opinions of Tristram Shandy, Gentleman'. Sterne himself departed this mortal plane in London on the eighth day of March 1768 (although no reports of his anxiously scribbling phantom have thus far been reported) However, his early years were spent in the local area and following his ordination as deacon he acted as vicar of the nearby village of Sutton-on-the-Forest and was also a prebendary of York Minster.

For a while (it seems unclear as to exactly how long) he lived down what is now the bustling hive of retail iniquity that is Stonegate, but in those halcyon pre-leisure retail days of old it was the centre of York's printing press trade, the first pioneering business having arrived in 1480.

The perceptive reader that I am confident you are will be pondering on the efficacy of this location for a future author and as such will forgive a small digression from our tale of the supernatural to honour the achievement of one of York's more notable sons.

Sterne duly took advantage of his locale in 1759 when deciding to self publish the first two parts of his now famous novel. Having been, as it would appear is the case with all aspiring novel writers, rejected by all the London publishers, Sterne dug into his own pockets and commissioned Anne Ward's printing business (publisher of York's principle daily newspaper the *York Courant*[1]) to produce the first two volumes. This would ultimately engender a nine part series published by London latecomer Robert Dodsley, the resultant success propelling its author to fame throughout Europe.

An element of the book's writing style has the narrator frequently breaking from the primary narrative to engage in a variety of musings with the reader, and that critical retrospective has lauded our celebrated man of the cloth as the ancestor of 'stream of consciousness fiction'. It is, in my humble opinion, amusing to note that the success of the novel resulted in two additional volumes of fictional sermons written by one of the book's early characters, a certain Parson Yorick, whose origin is a further manifestation of the author's desire for the book to be based upon his own life experiences. Surely then our most innovative of scribes is also responsible for the origination of the 'spin off' series.

My digression over, let us return to Sterne's abode, wherein he was repeatedly and regularly disturbed by a loud banging noise emanating from his immediate neighbour's dwelling. Finding no source for this irksome commotion he enquired of the local residents and was told that the previous owner of the property had been an old man living in fear of a late night intrusion by various brigands. At the moment the Minster bells had ceased their midnight tolling he had taken to deterring these imagined characters by repeatedly banging his walking stick on the wall next to his bed, the resultant combination of excessive fear and the incessant repetitiveness of the act culminating in the noise continuing even after the poor wretch had died.

It must be stated, however, that this was not by the hand of any dastardly intruder but the impassive progress of time, a mistress to which none are afforded protection, no matter the lofty position of their eminence.

---

1.   A four page folio published in partnership with George Peacock. Anne Ward had taken over the print business earlier that year as a result of her husband Caesar's demise.

THOMAS GENT

Illustration from an autobiography entitled The Life of Mr. Thomas Gent, Printer, of York, *published in 1746.*
Mezzotint by V. Green after an on an Oil Painting by N. Drake

Alluded to within what I sincerely hope is the diverting prose that constitutes our article on The Red Devil is the entrance to Coffee Yard, named for accommodating York's original coffeehouse in the seventeenth century. The area subsequently accommodated the print business owned by printer and publisher Thomas Gent and, if the reader will indulge our desire for continuity of theme, we hereby present enlightenment as to the particulars of this most notable historical inhabitant.

Born in Ireland in 1693, Gent is often described as eccentric, although in truth the man's only eccentric element appears to be the rather charmingly naive woodcuts he produced for his various publications. Although apprenticed as a printer in Dublin in his youth the unfortunate nature of an initiation rite for a printer by the name of Mears in Blackfriars, London seems to have created a temporary antipathy toward the industry and he left to become a labourer.[1]

Patently recovering his wits, Gent moved to York shortly after and took up employment with John White, no less a gentleman than the King's printer for York. During this period he became acquainted with Alice Guy, the upper maiden to his employer's wife Grace and became decidedly smitten with her. Unfortunately for our hapless suitor she decided to marry Charles Bourne, the grandson of John White. Far be it for us to assume any kind of lofty judgement appertaining to the proceedings, but with Alice being in the employ of Bourne's grandfather it is not beyond the realm of possibility that the poor girl was in some way deferential in her decision. But none alive today were there to bear witness so we must, in all good conscience, assume that she was a willing participant in the matrimonial arrangement.

That said, upon the demise of Mr Bourne in 1724 Alice appeared, some might say rather disrespectfully, to waste no time in hurrying Gent's return to York and marrying him. As such, Gent acquired the print business that he'd always aspired to and as a result assumed responsibility for York's first newspaper, the *York Mercury*.[2]

At this juncture we must cast our minds northwards to the mighty city of Newcastle, wherein lay the established print business of none other than John White the younger, son of John and Grace and publisher of the *Newcastle Courant*. Decidedly irked by the circamstances that resulted in Gent taking over the family business in York as opposed to himself, White Jr. happened upon the notion of establishing his own print business and publishing a rival paper entitled (rather unimaginatively) the *York Courant*.[3]

Consequently Gent, who although an experienced tradesman was, by judgement of his peers, a bit rubbish, became painfully aware of the potential for his fortunes to decline, a feeling no doubt exacerbated by the death of his and Alice's only child in 1726. By way of response he began to write and publish historical works; The *York Mercury* ceased publication in 1728 but *A History of York* appeared in 1730, two years after and with further histories of Ripon and Hull following in 1733 and 1735 respectively. In addition, 1734 was blessed with the publication of *Miscellanea Curiosa Or Entertainments For The Ingenious Of Both Sexes*. Or not so blessed as the publication was a commercial failure.

As was originally feared, the period after 1740 saw a diminishing of Gent's status and after suffering the loss of his lease on both the print premises and also his house Thomas Gent was forced to move to a residence in nearby Petergate where his publishing output significantly decreased. A number of publications covered religious themes and poetry and he became known for his output of chapbooks.[4]

At the risk of generating a morbid state of melancholy amongst those readers with a more sensitive disposition it must be duly documented that the ill-fated Thomas Gent's fortunes did not improve. Following the passing of his cherished Alice on the first day of April 1761 his income continued to decline and he suffered from ill-health. Benefactors in the form of friends allowed him to continue what had become a somewhat miserable existence, until he joined Alice on the nineteenth day of 1778 and was buried opposite York Minster at St Michael-le-Belfry.

---

1. According to Gent's memoirs the right seems to have been instigated by the 'chapel' , an internal brotherhood common amongst printers at the time and whose role was to establish regulations to maintain the employees discipline: '...I was obliged to submit to that immemorial custom, the origin of which they could not then explain to me. It commenced by walking round the chapel ... singing an alphabetical anthem, tuned literally to the vowels; striking me, kneeling, with a broadsword; and pouring ale upon my head: my titles were exhibited much to this effect, 'Thomas Gent, baron of College Green, earl of Fingall, with power to the limits of Dublin bar, captain general of the Teagues, near the Lake of Allen, and lord high admiral over all the bogs in Ireland.' To confirm which, and that I might not pay over again for the same ceremony, through forgetfulness, they allowed me godfathers, the first I ever had before... and these, my new pious fathers, were the un-reverend Mr. Holt and Mr. Palmer.'

2. The inaugural issue of *The York Mercury* was published in February 1719 by John White's wife, Grace, who inherited the print business after her husband's death.

3. Established in Stonegate, the first issue of the *York Courant* was published in either August or September 1725.

4. Chapbooks came into being in the sixteenth century as a result of booklet printing becoming affordable and were chiefly used for the dissemination of popular culture amongst the less privileged members of society.

The EBOR GHOST

Taken by no lesser a person than York's Ghostfinder General Rachel Lacy and in the presence of her associate Diana Jarvis the photograph was, appropriately, taken during the 2005 York Ghost Festival. The location of this eerie photograph is the Ebor tavern in Bishopthorpe where Ms Lacy and Ms Jarvis were about to partake of some refreshment during the proceeds of the festival.

Ever vigilant as to the potential presence of spirits Ms Lacy decided upon the use of her camera by way of attempting to capture any presence that may have been in the room. Pointing it towards the main area in front of the their table, Ms Lacy was providential enough in her timing to capture the form of a gentleman reflected in the mirror on the opposite wall. The profile of Ms Jarvis can also be seen passing in front of the spectre, who is bending over the beer pumps at the bar. It must be reiterated that Ms Lacy and Ms Jarvis war the only two people in the room at the time.

The landlord of the Ebor was shown the photograph in an attempt to identify the gentleman in question but neither he, nor any members of his staff, nor any of his regular visitors to the tavern had any idea as to who this person may be.

As will always be the case when imparting news of photographic evidence we beseech our discerning readers to embark upon their own assessment as to the veracity of the image and further any comments and opinions to the editorial address.

Detail of the photograph taken in the Ebor public house in Bishopthorpe.
By Rachel Lacy

The COMMON HALL LANE GHOST

f feel it incumbent upon me to warn you, dear reader, that the following tale may leave you wondering exactly what kind of unearthly manifestations are existing within the heart of York.

That said, I fear I may have unwittingly cast doubt upon the noble and audacious nature of our patrons, of which I am most humbly apologetic. As such, with no further ado, lest us allow our thoughts to move in the direction of the resplendent structure that is known as the Guildhall, itself the location of a number of spectral manifestations and therefore a subject that we will undoubtedly be returning to in greater detail in a future edition.

Originally a fifteenth-century structure forged as an assembly location for the York guilds, the original building, alas, was largely destroyed by the Second World War 'Baedeker air raid' in 1942. Not wishing to allow such an unsporting act of demolition to impede the smooth functioning of York's commerce it was rebuilt and duly opened with great pomp and ceremony by Queen Elizabeth The Queen Mother in 1960.

A compelling but little known attribute of the Guildhall is the track known as Common Hall Lane; mediaeval in origin it runs from a watergate at the edge of the River Ouse, beneath the northern part of the Guildhall and orientates in the direction of Saint Helen's Square.

In January of 2017 the local history group York Past And Present were undertaking one of their recurrent and most exemplary tours of the Guildhall when an experience left them notably discombobulated. Following the group's congregation in a nearby tavern, where it must be made clear at this juncture that no more hardy a brew was partaken than coffee, they set off to participate in the routine that has proved most successful on previous occasions. The time was eleven in the morning and following the customary and concise historical outline of the hall the group proceeded to fulfil their accustomed route.

With the Guildhall clock chiming its midday notification the gathering of inquisitive souls headed towards the finale of the tour. Common Hall Lane beckoned! A doorway blocks the entrance to the lane which, once negotiated, leads to a small circular stairway and then to the lane itself. At the far end of the lane is a gate that blocks any form of passage to the River Ouse. At the head of our intrepid party was Sue Hogarth, who, having a clear view of an unencumbered prospect took full advantage by taking a photograph.

Some time later, secure in the comfort of her own abode, Ms. Hogarth was perusing her tour photographs prior to making them available to other members via the club's journal.[1]

Studying the image of Common Lane, she could see that up ahead, silhouetted by the rays of light streaming in

The Entrance To Common Hall Lane
By Sue Bingham, *York Past & Present*

from the River Ouse entrance, were three cloaked figures. Further scrutiny revealed that in addition to the inexplicable figures there was, conversely, a complete absence of the gate, as if, for the briefest of moments during the taking of the photograph, the gate had dissolved to allow for the appearance of our spectral individuals.

I have absolutely no doubt that you, our most undaunted of readers, will wish to undertake a full and scholastic appraisal of the photograph without fear of impunity and it is therefore reproduced for your consideration upon this very page.

"It was the last section of the tour. Everyone in the group were waiting to come down the stairs into Common Hall Lane and while it was quiet and no one was around I thought I would get a photo.

It was empty. There was only the tour leader and myself there. So I took the shot. All I could see was the tunnel and the light from the river end.

I certainly never saw any silhouettes or figures. It wasn't until I got home and looked at the picture that I realised the figures were there."

Sue Bingham. From the York Mix article
published 9 February, 2015.

1.   http://www.yorkmix.com/life/history/is-this-a-photograph-of-ghosts-under-york-guildhall/

COMPLETE WALK

The three walks combined

1. Hole in the Wall
2. Precentor's Court
3. York Minster
4. Guy Fawkes Inn
5. The Treasurer's House
6. Grays Court
7. The Royal Oak
8. The Golden Slipper
9. St William's College
10. 5 College Street
11. Snickleway Inn
12. Bedern
13. Black Swan
14. St Saviour
15. Golden Fleece
16. Shambles
17. Old White Swan
18. Holy Trinity Church
19. Roman Bath
20. All Saints' Church
21. York Dungeon
22. Clifford's Tower

23. The York Barguest
24. York Castle Museum
25. Cock and Bottle
26. The Whippet Inn
27. Priory Church of the Holy Trinity
28. Micklegate Bar
29. Lendal Cellars
30. Guildhall
31. Common Hall Lane Ghost
32. Judge's Court
33. Thomas Gent
34. The Red Devil
35. Haunting of Laurence Sterne
36. Stonegate
37. Ye Olde Starre Inne
38. Punchbowl
39. The Yorkshire Museum
40. The King's Manor
41. York Theatre Royal
42. Dean Court Hotel
43. The York Arms

A GUIDED WALK
AROUND THE STREETS
AND TAVERNS OF

HAUNTED YORK

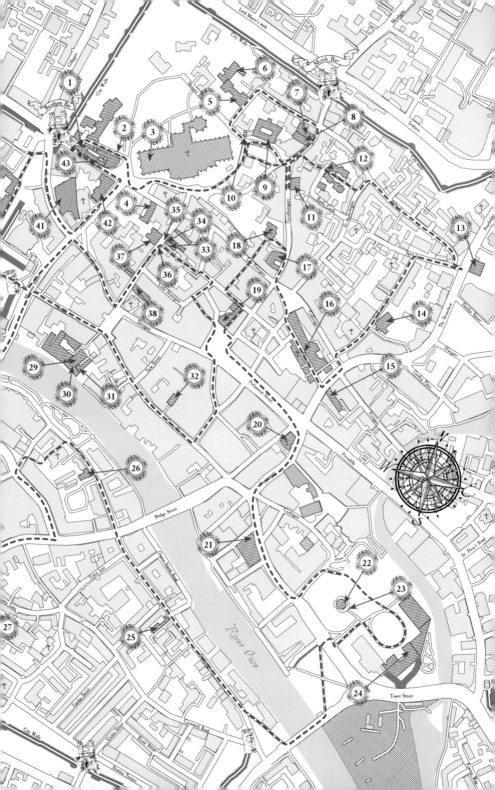

NOTES

GUIDE TO THE MAPS

1. Were you to undertake the individual walks (maps 1 and 2) rather than the complete walk (map 3) you will, inevitably, re-encounter streets and buildings that you have already become familiar with from a previous walk. That said, should you choose to embark upon the tavern walk as your inaugural adventure you may have no memory of anything.

PRECENTOR'S COURT

1. M.J Wayland has written number of books about ghosts including two concerning York. His website can be found at: http://mjwayland.com

THE TREASURER'S HOUSE

1. Constructed in the shadow of York Minster itself, the Treasurer's House was originally built to function as the home of the Minster's Treasurer, it's nom de plume suggesting that however resplendent the city's history it appeared to have little impact on the imaginative inclination of its inhabitants. The foremost such favoured gentleman was Radulphus, appointed in 1091 and followed in 1109 by William Fitz Herbert who, it would appear, was in residency when the building succumbed to the onslaught of the fire.

GRAYS COURT

1. The highs and lows of Helen Heraty and her families struggle with their dream project are chronicled in the film *Folie á Deux* by labour of Love Films. For more information, visit their website: https://www.laboroflovefilms.com/hotelfolly

ST WILLIAM'S COLLEGE

1. A chantry was a medieval endowment created for a priest or priests to celebrate a sung mass for the soul of a particular person, This was usualy the individual who had established the fund.

BEDERN

1. This was to allow the clergyman access to the Minster without the need to mix with the ruffians that made up York's population.
2. *York and the North Riding*, published in 1857, p486.

PRIORY CHURCH OF THE HOLY TRINITY

1. An exciting tale that paints a fascinating picture of the abbess as a sword wielding Amazon that succeeds in despatching a number of soldiers before

succumbing to overwhelming odds. The only modification to the story is that it is set during the Civil War, rather than the Reformation.

JUDGE'S COURT

1. Now a hotel, one assumes that the marketing necessary for it to be a success in its new capacity will bring it to more people's attention.
2. From 1806 the judges were accommodated at the nearby Judge's Lodgings.

ALL SAINTS' CHURCH

1. Extending to the very walls of York the Forest contained sixty villages within one hundred thousand acres, the largest being Easingwold at a distance of about 12 miles.

SHAMBLES

1. Should you choose to visit the shrine, please bear in mind that the buildings in Shambles were re-numbered in the eighteenth century, a fact unknown at the time of establishing Margaret's home as a place of veneration. As such, it is likely that her actual home was in the property opposite, a theory in part substantiated by its still existing priest hole.

YORK MINSTER

1. This building burned to the ground along with St Peter's School in 741.

HAUNTED TAVERNS

1. The walk has been designed to be circular, so that you can, effectively, start where you choose and still finish where you started. Or not finish at all.

THE GOLDEN SLIPPER

1. The reports became so common that Northampton Museum created a Concealed Shoe Index that by 2012 had gathered 1900 entries. As with the Golden Slipper, the majority of finds are of single shoes and about half of them belonged to children.

YE OLDE STARRE INNE

1. So as to avoid a potential faux pas it should be noted that the 'Ye' is a pseudo-archaic use of the Elder Fuþark rune know as 'Thorn'. Originally it looked more like a letter 'P' but then became to look pretty much the same as a 'Y'. It is, however pronounced 'th'. Therefore the pronunciation of 'Ye' is 'the'.

SNICKLEWAY INN

1. Available from all good bookshops.

ASIDES and DON'T STRAY FROM THE PATH

A64 MALTON ROAD

1. A report compiled by the Rev. Lionel Fanthorpe, a Cardiff based vicar who is has also spent many decades investigating strange phenomena.

ST GEORGE'S FIELD

1. Immortalised by the artist Andrew Howat for an edition of the British weekly magazine *Look and Learn*.

ST MARY'S CHURCH

1. Not helped by the news that his relative had been arrested for the heinous crime of being in debt, and that the debt was actually Calverley's responsibility.

2. The circumstances of Walter Calverley's crime and punishment became so notorious that two stage plays were written dramatising it: *The Miseries of Enforced Marriage*, written in 1607 by George Wilkins, and *A Yorkshire Tragedy*, written a year later by William Shakespeare (although his authorship has been disputed).

BAR CONVENT

1. There is apparently a second surviving hand of Margaret Clitherow housed at the Ladyewell Shrine in Preston in Lancashire.

NATIONAL RAILWAY MUSEUM

1. At the time of writing they are still available to be viewed at: https://blog.nrm.org.uk/halloween-at-the-museum

DAVYGATE

1. Detailed in a 2002 field report of an archeological watching brief, the prehistoric material that is a rare find in central York had not been confirmed as Iron Age but was thought to belong to that period

EPILOGUE

We hope you've enjoyed your tour around the ghost infested ancient streets of York but please bear in mind that this is by no means an exhaustive account. Our intention is to expand on the contents of *Haunted York* in future editions and for this we need your help.

If you've had a spectral encounter in York, or if you have any knowledge of ghosts that haven't been covered in these pages, or you wish to add or correct any of the details within the book, please contact me via the publisher.

Thanks must go to Rachel Lacy, York's 'Ghost Finder General' and also a Paranormal Historian. Rachel runs the Paranormal and Spectral Investigations (PSI) group which has been going since 2003 and is also one of the co-founders of the York Ghost Festival.